# Confronting Educational Issues

## Decision Making with Case Studies

Francis X. Russo

*The University of Rhode Island*

**KENDALL/HUNT PUBLISHING COMPANY**
2460 Kerper Boulevard   P.O. Box 539   Dubuque, Iowa 52004-0539

To my son, Gregory, from whose life and death I learned my most painful lessons in decision making.

# Contents

# Preface

*Case Studies and Decision-Making Skills.* The need for their students to practice decision-making skills, such as critical thinking and problem solving, has long been accepted as a major goal of teacher preparation programs, and case studies have been found to be an effective vehicle to attain this end. By challenging students to make decisions on controversial issues arising from the day-to-day operations of the educational enterprise, case studies provide the practical testing ground for the theoretical and conceptual knowledge that students have mastered in academic and professional courses. Students change from passive learners to active "doers and thinkers" using the power of analysis to eliminate some possibilities, the process of deduction to practice making inferences, the process of rigorous inquiry and reasoning to recognize substantive issues and to support hunches, and the power of intellectual persuasion to influence others and acquire support.

*Purpose of Book.* It is the purpose of this book of case studies, to address this need to develop decision-making skills by challenging students—whether novices or experienced educators—to practice making decisions that require them to think analytically, carefully, and understandingly about the experiences the cases describe. These cases involve a wide variety of educational issues of a controversial nature and reflect the realities of public education in America with the conflicting economic, social, and political forces that determine so much of what happens in the educational enterprise. The situations presented in the cases are neither simple nor capable of easy solution. They include a unique blending of philosophical, ethical, and technical issues complicated by the prejudices, attitudes, and sentiments of the people involved. To reach a decision concerning these situations, students are led to strive—through reflection and critical thinking—to understand as fully as possible not only the economic, political, and social factors governing the situations but the people involved in them and the outcomes that result when these people emphasize certain values and avoid others.

*Approach to Case Studies.* This book utilizes a variation of the case problem and case study techniques. Each of the cases presents the problems and issues, the facts bearing on them, the background information, and brief sketches of the leading personalities. These cases are vignettes of incidents drawn from the every-day world of elementary, secondary, and higher education; the cases trace the incidents, not their ramifications or outcomes.

Each case allows for vicarious experiencing in which students learn about, but do not directly participate in, an actual experience and in which they have the opportunity to think through the specific problem focused upon by the secondary experience. Students are expected to become familiar with the problems involved, to identify with the persons confronted by the issues, and to raise questions and develop answers that are relevant to the decision being made. This requires students to use such decision-making skills as critical thinking and problem solving, employing a coherent, constructive, generalized questioning structure that will allow them to conceptualize issues, to understand the complexity of the problem, and to design a plan of action. As they exercise these skills, students develop an "ear" for decision making: evidence is considered, individual ideas are presented, judgments are made, and a viewpoint is defended.

After students have arrived at a clear conception of how they view the issues, their implications, and possible approaches to them, they should pursue further understanding and guidance through outside readings, library research, and related materials from other disciplines. Case studies, then, provide students with two unique learning opportunities: first, to develop an "ear" for decision making, a critical dimension of intellectual life; and second, to practice critical thinking and to improve problem-solving skills by operating upon problems arising out of the human situation with the ideas, insights, and concepts acquired from readings, lectures, class discussions, and life experiences.

*Use of Case Studies Book.* This book is comprised of an introduction, the case studies, and study guides for each case. The introduction suggests steps students should follow in their approach to the problems    raised   by the case and cautions against pitfalls they should   avoid  in the process of decision-making. The case studies include   issues that evolve around such areas as regionalization, moral misconduct,    accountability,   burnout,   cheating,   teacher/pupil sexual orientation, home schooling, cultural pluralism, disadvantaged students, teacher preparation, discipline, gifted children, parental rights vs. *parens patriae,* religious observance, racial conflict, testing/grading, teacher injury, and mainstreaming. The study guides provide direction, facilitate student involvement, and aid the instructor in focusing upon issues.

This book should be used in both foundations and methods courses. The cases offer actual situations that give meaning to the normative and philosophic issues considered in a foundations course and to the methodological choices raised in a methods course. This book should also prove useful as a supplementary text in introductory undergraduate education courses and in graduate courses that examine issues in contemporary American education. It will add a needed enriching experience: helping students to bridge the gap between theory and practice and preparing them for field-work experiences. It will lend itself to whatever approach an instructor employs. [An instructor's manual is available from the publisher without charge.] Case studies may be used to introduce, develop, or summarize concepts, issues, etc. They may be adapted to a variety of teaching and learning strategies from role playing, debating, and group discussions to research papers and sundry forms of written assignments. They may be assigned to individual students or to the class as a whole, and they may be singled out to be examined periodically as the course develops or studied as a group during a segment of the semester.

*One final note. . . .* Since I wrote my first casebook (*The Right May Be Wrong*) two years ago, my colleagues, who have adopted it for classroom use, have provided me with invaluable feedback as to its weaknesses and strengths. I am grateful for their constructive criticisms, and I have sought to incorporate their suggestions in this new casebook.

The goal of this casebook remains the same as in my last one. It is to encourage students confronted with educational issues and problems to master those skills and abilities necessary for responsible, effective decision making. Again, it remains my hope that a high degree of such mastery will be achieved so that future choices made in education will resolve existent problems rather than create new ones.

# Acknowledgments

I wish to express my appreciation to Frank M. Perry (URI) for his suggestions and assistance during the preparation of this manuscript and to William Woodward (URI), Rae O'Neill (URI), and Patricia Kelly (URI) for their timely comments and support. Special thanks also go to Mackie Robinson for her skill and care in typing this manuscript and for her thoughtfulness in attending to the many other matters required for the preparation of this manuscript.

# Introduction

*Theory-Practice Dichotomy.* Throughout their history, teacher preparation programs have been plagued by a theory-practice dichotomy, that is, a sharp division between institutional-based courses with requirements that provide theoretical and conceptual knowledge and field-based courses with requirements that provide ongoing and immediate practical-teaching experience. The problem created by this dichotomy has led to the practice of dividing the learning experience for students interested in the area of education into two phases. Phase one encompasses extensive academic and professional course work on campus that precedes field work experiences. It focuses upon the *supra-deductive* dimension of learning with the mastering of theory and the interpreting of experience in terms of the theory. Phase two encompasses a limited period of supervised training in the classroom that comes after the academic course work. It focuses upon the *infra-inductive* dimension of learning with experiential learning and the development of ideas evolving from the experience.

While educators rarely question the importance of both these aspects of learning, students frequently complain that what has been learned in college does not seem to equip them with the necessary abilities and skills to face and resolve the real problems encountered in the classroom. Students discover that these real problems, unlike their course work on campus, demand they engage in such decision-making skills as critical thinking (analysis, deduction, inquiry, etc.) and problem solving. They find they are required to develop these skills if they are to identify each problem, question how it occurred, define the issues involved, weigh possible solutions, and develop and implement a course of action to resolve it.

*Teaching and Decision Making.* The very nature of the tasks of teaching—shaping curriculum, choosing instructional materials, controlling classroom environment, interacting with students, parents, administrators—require teachers to engage constantly in the process of selecting between two or more alternative courses of action. Often these choices are difficult, and teachers find their decision-making skills being challenged by educational problems that are complex and ambiguous, reflecting a unique blend of philosophical, ethical, and technical questions. Consequently, few in the teaching profession will deny that decision making is a critical aspect of their work and the most fundamental of all teaching skills that must be developed.

*Decision-Making Skills and This Casebook.* This casebook addresses the need to develop the teaching skills of decision making. It presents experiences that require students to make specific decisions using the process of inquiry and reflection and practicing the analytical sifting of pros and cons. The cases in this book should appeal to the student's theoretic instinct, what William James defined as the need to learn causes, reasons, and abstract conceptions. They should provide ample opportunities for students to practice and develop such analytical skills as judging the credibility of a source, inferring explanations, validating an observation, supporting an argument, and identifying underlying assumptions.

These cases, involve a wide variety of educational issues of a controversial nature. They present issues that have confronted the schools throughout all times as well as issues that have been spawned by social, economic, and political factors unique to the present time. Each case brings a segment of reality into the classroom by introducing problems drawn from actual situations. Students struggle with the stubborn facts that must be faced in any real-life situation. They are confronted with the inequities that can result from the politics of school systems and with the injustices arising from instances of unfairness by administrators, of incompetence by teachers, of self-serving by parents, politicians and interest groups, and of thoughtlessness by students. Each case, then, is a record of a complex situation that provides students with the opportunity to learn to approach educational dilemmas by identifying issues, organizing possible strategies, considering negative and positive outcomes, and proposing specific solutions to address the problem.

*"Ear" for Decision Making Developed.* Each case provides an opportunity for vicarious experiencing with all its unique advantages. Students learn about an actual experience without directly participating in it, and they think through the specific problems which the secondary experience focuses upon. This entails that students do more than passively listen. Rather, they engage in such decision-making skills as critical thinking and problem solving, employing a coherent,

constructive, generalized questioning structure to conceptualize issues, to understand the complexity of the problem, and to design a plan of action. As they exercise these skills, they develop an "ear" for decision making, and evidence is considered, individual ideas are presented, judgments are made, and a viewpoint is defended.

*Suggested Steps in Decision Making.* In the role of decision maker, a student's approach to the problems raised by each case should follow four steps:

1. identify and state clearly the meaningful issues involved;

2. define his/her position on each issue;

3. weigh the implications of alternative approaches to each issue;

4. make a decision and formulate a course of action to implement it.

In effect, the student should ask four questions:

1. What are the issues I find important to this case?

2. What is my position on these issues?

3. What are the advantages or disadvantages if I select one approach to these issues as against another?

4. On the basis of these issues and my position on them, what action would I take as decision maker?

*Pitfalls to avoid: Steps 1 and 2.* Each step or related question has certain pitfalls the student should avoid. In step one, facts and minutiae should not be identified as issues. For example, in the case of *Stephen Lowe*, Stephen's illegitimacy and Ms. Lowe's failure to marry are points of fact and not issues. An issue might be: Should a counselor's services be distributed equally among all advisees or should they be focused upon those few with specific needs and problems? In step two, all facets of an issue should be analyzed before a position is taken on it. Again in the case of *Stephen Lowe*, the student should not take a stand on retaining Stan as Stephen's counselor simply on the basis of the effectiveness of the relationship and networking bond resulting from Stan's rapport with Stephen. Rather, the student must also carefully consider the less favorable impact Stan's work with Stephen has upon Stan's relationship and networking bond with his other advisees and their parents, with the other teachers, and with Mae Watterson. Similarly, consideration must be given to the less favorable impact Stan's work with Stephen has upon Stephen's relationship and networking bond with his mother, with his classmates, and with his other teachers.

*Pitfalls to avoid: Steps 3 and 4.* In step three, the implications of each approach to an issue should be fully explored. Again, in the case of *Stephen Lowe*, a decision by the school to ignore Ms. Lowe's request to replace Stan may be viewed in sharply different ways. It may be viewed as a proper extension of the concept of *parens patriae,* i.e., the state's paternalistic right to intervene and provide guardianship for minors and, consequently, as an appropriate approach to the issue. It also may be viewed as an undermining of the rights of the parent and the privacy and independence of the family, and, consequently, as a highly inappropriate approach. In step four, the course of action selected should be consistent with the decision made, specifying practical measures to carry it out. Again in the case of *Stephen Lowe*, if the student decides to replace Stan as counselor, then the student must also prepare a blueprint of the measures to be taken that will allow for the exchange of counselors without causing further conflict and emotional distress and that will promote new, constructive, fruitful relationships and networking bonds among all parties involved.

*Use of Other Sources.* In following the above four steps and avoiding the consequent pitfalls, students utilize their "ear" for decision-making as they analyze the case and identify issues. Once they have arrived at a clear conception of how they view the issues, their implications, and possible approaches to them, then they should pursue further understanding and guidance through outside readings, community resources, library research, and related materials from other disciplines. Thus, case studies provide the students with two unique learning opportunities: first, to develop an "ear" for decision making, a critical dimension of intellectual life; and, second, to practice critical thinking and to improve problem-solving skills by operating upon problems arising out of the human situation with the ideas, insights, and concepts acquired from readings, lectures, class discussions, and life experiences.

*Tool for Group Discussions.* The cases should contribute to rich and productive experiences in group discussions. Each case provides a focus and a framework (common information about issues, problems, personalities, etc.) upon which the members of the group develop a variety of viewpoints and interpretations. As members share and consider the various ways of looking at a problem, they develop a flexible attitude toward the beliefs of others and a firm commitment and integrity toward their own. They become aware of the value of cooperative thinking and acting, and they become cognizant of the significance of meaningful, two-way communication. In effect, they develop a commitment to the practice of thinking analytically by looking at problems through the eyes of others and, in turn, seeking to understand the pressures others operate under and their possible biases, motives, and opinions.

*Student/Teacher Roles Altered.* The use of cases alters the roles of students and teacher in the classroom. Students as decision makers in case studies abandon their common role of being passive and become active participants primarily responsible for the direction and success of the learning experience. They are the "doers and thinkers", and it is their analyses, their conclusions, and their systematic, rigorous, and efficient approach to problems that dominate the class session. Teachers as collaborators in class discussions of cases shed their stereotyped image of being authoritarian and play a non-directive role, leaving decisions primarily to the students. They create a learning environment of openness and trust that is supportive of student needs and responsive to student uncertainties. In all interactions with students, they demonstrate such qualities of democratic leadership as restraint, understanding, patience, timing, knowledge, and clear judgment.

*Nature of Case Studies Examined.* This book utilizes a variation of the case problem and case study techniques. Each of the cases presents the problems and issues, the facts bearing on them, the background information, and brief sketches of the leading personalities. These cases are vignettes of incidents drawn from the everyday world of elementary, secondary, and higher education; the cases trace the incidents, not their ramifications or outcomes. The cases comprise a collection of problems derived from the author's personal experiences and the experiences of others with whom he has worked in the field of education over the past thirty-five years. They include issues that evolve around such areas as: regionalization, moral misconduct, accountability, burnout, cheating, teacher/pupil sexual orientation, home schooling, cultural pluralism, disadvantaged students, teacher preparation, discipline, gifted children, parental rights vs. *parens patriae,* religious observance, racial conflict, testing/grading, teacher injury, and mainstreaming. Every effort has been made to disguise the people and the places that formed the basis for these cases. While any similarity to actual persons or places is strictly accidental, such similarity is also highly indicative of the universality and applicability of the cases.

*Study Guides and Manual Provided.* To assist the students in the decision-making process, this book contains a study guide for each case. The study guide assists in examining the case by suggesting an area of concern, concepts, questions, and reference materials relevant to the case. It provides questions, terms, and references that should be considered and built upon as the case is analyzed and a decision is made. To assist the instructor in the classroom use of this casebook, a manual has also been developed and is available from the publisher without charge. This manual focuses upon the content of the cases and upon methodology to be used in teaching the cases. It outlines the steps to be followed in examining the cases, lists the areas to be explored for possible issues in each case, and suggests specific teaching approaches appropriate to each case.

*One final note. . . .* One final note in closing: since this is a casebook, no attempt has been made to provide answers nor to suggest rules and regulations that will result in specific decisions. The nature of each case is such that answers are obscure and solutions in doubt. Students will discover that what they consider to be the "right" decision or solution may well be rejected as being the "wrong" one by colleagues whose examination of the same problem has resulted in an opposing position. Obviously, a multitude of conflicting answers and solutions are possible. Students may find such uncertainty disquieting, but this does not diminish the educational worth of analyzing cases. For while the case study experience promotes the confusion of conflicting decisions, it also develops habits of mind such as being well-informed, viewing things from another person's perspective, being open-minded, and not making a decision when evidence is insufficient.

# The Kiss

Frank Kaprian was a quiet workhorse-type of teacher who fulfilled his teaching responsibilities methodically, efficiently, and effectively. As a member of the math department at Trent High School, he rarely missed a day of school, was always prepared for classes, demanded quality work, imposed rigorous grading standards, and maintained orderly, disciplined, responsive classes. Kaprian had received an excellent education that included advanced degrees in math and computer science. He taught ninth grade Algebra, senior honors courses in advanced math, and was advisor to the math team. He was popular with the students who found him to be fair but firm, knowledgeable but humble, and concerned but patient. He was respected by his colleagues for his teaching skills and admired for his quiet, unobtrusive polite manner.

Trent High School was located in the placid, middle-class community of Locklan Heights, a predominantly white suburban town fifty miles north of a major east coast city. Over the past fifteen years, Locklan Heights had opened its doors to commercial and industrial business with several newly-constructed, high-rise buildings housing major regional insurance companies and research offices for national conglomerates. Many of Trent High School's fourteen hundred students were children of the professionals who worked in these office complexes. There college-educated parents were deeply concerned with the quality of the school's educational offerings.

Trent had a strong academic program that easily met the state Regent Standards; it offered a rich variety of college and honors courses, and it required students to attain high levels of skills competence and subject matter mastery in all courses taught. Trent's principal, who had the distinction of holding this position longer than any of his predecessors, was Sheldon Wimple. He had been a vigorous, effective administrator when he first arrived at the school twenty-two years ago, and under his leadership Trent had developed a quality curriculum and a well-trained, committed staff of teachers. But over the years, Wimple changed dramatically. He became increasingly compromising, vacillating on issues, avoiding conflict with faculty and parents, and referring all problems that could not be safely ignored to the superintendent's office. As this policy of inaction and non-involvement gradually pervaded all administrative decisions, faculty concluded that Wimple was simply biding his time until his retirement, and they referred to him derisively as "Wimpy."

Shortly after Frank Kaprian had graduated from college, he married Julia Santon, his childhood sweetheart. Julia was a delicate and beautiful woman who suffered from a congenital heart disease that severely limited her activity. She had been warned not to have a child, but she knew Frank wanted one and, after several miscarriages and a difficult pregnancy, she gave birth to a daughter, Maria. The Kaprians were a happy, loving, inseparable family who always supported one another and shared life's joys and sorrows. Frank was a dedicated and thoughtful husband catering to his wife's needs and avoiding social events at school or with his colleagues that she was unable to attend.

In the spring before their twentieth wedding anniversary, Julia Kaprian succumbed to the heart condition that had plagued her throughout her life. Frank was devastated by her death; in his depressed and despondent state, he was unable to conduct classes properly or to meet with the math team. This led parents and students to complain to Principal Wimple and to demand that another teacher be assigned to assist Kaprian. Wimple, who was anxious both to satisfy these demands and to avoid antagonizing older, tenured faculty with an overload of additional duties, responded by assigning Marjorie Hecht, a young, newly-appointed teacher to help Kaprian coach the math team and meet his other teaching responsibilities.

Hecht, a first-year teacher, was bright, enthusiastic and blessed with a pleasant and ingratiating manner. She felt compassion for Kaprian in his time of grief and devoted herself fully to her additional duties without complaining. She worked with Kaprian during her unassigned periods and after school hours, helping him to complete records, grade tests, review materials, and prepare lessons. She scheduled practice sessions for the math team and helped Kaprian to prepare the team for its remaining matches. During this period Hecht was drawn very close to Kaprian and became deeply involved in his personal life. He confided in her, lamenting his loss, and she listened, supported, encouraged, and comforted him until he was able to cope with his crisis of grief and overcome his despondency.

The following September, Kaprian resumed his full teaching responsibilities, but he continued to share coaching the math team with Hecht. The math team's performance under Kaprian had been adequate, but with Hecht as co-advisor it became exceptional. Hecht seemed to breathe a new *espirit de corps* into the group: the brightest students—female as well as male—tried out for the team; competition for positions was keen; and frequently held practice sessions were always fully attended. Buy the spring term the math team had won all of its matches and had been selected to represent the state in a three-day, regional, championship tournament to be held in Leviton, a coastal city located two hundred miles away.

On the evening before the tournament, the math team, with Kaprian and Hecht serving as advisors and chaperons, arrived at Leviton and occupied rooms at a hotel near the center of the city. At 1:30 A.M. the following morning, one of the students became ill; however, when the other students sought help, Kaprian and Hecht could not be found, and hotel officials brought in a doctor to tend to the student. Kaprian and Hecht did not return to their hotel rooms until 4:30 A.M., long after the student had received the necessary medical attention and was resting comfortably.

In spite of this distressful event, the students performed well in the tournament that day, and they returned to Locklan Heights as the regional champs. The students did not report the incident to their parents or to school officials. However, they did discuss it with their classmates, and Principle Wimple soon heard rumors that Kaprian and Hecht "secretly met to have sex" and left the math team unchaperoned when a sick student needed help. Wimple chose to ignore the rumors; he did not want to add to their credibility by acting on them in any way. He was anxious to avoid the unpleasantness of a confrontation with either parents or faculty which he feared would be triggered by any attempt to investigate a rumored incident involving faculty in a sex scandal and dereliction of duty. He chose not to discuss the incident with Kaprian until several weeks had passed and all rumors had faded. He found Kaprian to be candid and sincere, and he accepted his "regrets" over the incident and his assurances that "no sexual indiscretions had occurred."

The Kaprian-Hecht relationship abruptly ended in June when she accepted a higher paying position in a large city located across the country. The following September when school began, Kaprian found himself without companionship and very much alone. Hecht was gone, he had never cultivated meaningful social relationships with anyone on the faculty, and his daughter attended college out of state and returned home only on holidays.

Among the students in Kaprian's ninth grade algebra class was Barbara Racklin, a blue-eyed brunette of dazzling beauty, whose well-endowed, fully-developed body belied the youth and innocence of her fourteen years. Barbara's mother, a former state beauty queen, had divorced her husband shortly after the birth of her other daughter. Though she did not remarry, she did cohabitate with several local businessmen, and her children had experienced periodic changes of "live-in fathers" during their childhood. Mrs. Racklin was a shrewd, talented businesswomen who had parlayed the money and property received in her divorce settlement into a string of successful beauty salons. She was highly respected in the business community, served on the city's Chamber of Commerce, and was active in several business organizations that promoted the city's economic welfare.

Mrs. Racklin sought a close relationship with her children, tended to be overprotective of them, and encouraged them to confide in her. As a single-parent mother, she always felt an added responsibility for being available when her children needed her and for being attentive when they shared their problems with her. But she frequently had little time for her children because of the demands of business. Mrs. Racklin was proud of her children, and this pride was manifested in her efforts to enhance their appearances through fashionable clothes, carefully groomed hair styles, and whatever added glamour the skilled application of cosmetics could provide.

Barbara Racklin was unquestionably the most beautiful student at Trent High School. Male students flocked around her, female students envied her, and faculty in general, could not help but take note of her. But though her beauty and dress made her the center of attention, she remained aloof from male student advances, limited her social activities to membership in the cheerleaders' squad, and focused upon her school work. She was enrolled in a college track program, and teachers found her to be a quiet, polite, conscientious student of average ability who applied herself fully to all tasks assigned.

Math was not Barbara's strongest subject, but she knew that she must pass two years of it to meet college entrance requirements, and she was determined to earn a quality grade in algebra. She felt fortunate to have Kaprian as a teacher because his explanation of materials

4

was clear, his treatment was thorough, his pace was reasonable, and his quiet, concerned, patient manner was appealing. She was one of the few students who took advantage of his extra-credit review sessions which were held every Friday afternoon after school. By the end of the second quarter, she received a B+ and Kaprian, who had come to know her well and admired her diligence, praised and encouraged her.

As the term progressed, Kaprian found himself strangely attracted by this reticent beauty. She seemingly never invited his attention; yet, she possessed a bewitching charm that made it impossible for him to ignore her. She knew enough to let her beauty speak for itself and to avoid any clumsy, obvious, sexy mannerisms appropriate to an immature teenager. She was drawn to Kaprian; his erudition impressed her, his quiet, patient, manner brought her security, and his concerned but polite, reserved approach evoked feelings of trust and a curiosity to know him better.

On a Friday afternoon, shortly after the spring recess had ended, Kaprian dismissed his extra-credit, algebra-review class, gathered his materials, and walked to his car. As he crossed the teachers' parking lot, he noticed Barbara standing alone in the waiting area for late buses, and he offered to drive her home. Barbara accepted, sat in the front seat, and gave him directions to her house. She lived several miles away in a sparsely settled rural area at the edge of the city. During the fifteen-minute drive toward her home, Kaprian engaged in a light, pleasant conversation that was filled with good-natured teasing and witty remarks. In the banter that followed, Kaprian became enchanted by the warmth and charm of Barbara's shy laughter and beautiful, smiling face.

When they were approaching her home, Barbara had Kaprian stop the car to let her off at a wooded area a short distance from where she lived. Kaprian reached across the seat with his left hand to open her door, and as he did, he faced her directly with his lips a few inches from her mouth. He proceeded to embrace her with his right arm and to kiss her fully on the lips. Barbara slid her arms around his neck, and they remained embraced in a lingering kiss that lasted a few minutes. Kaprian then released her and opened the door. She gathered her books, which had fallen from her lap to the floor, and after mumbling a "thank you for the ride," closed the car door and walked to her house.

The following Monday morning, Principle Wimple received a phone call from an enraged Mrs. Racklin who demanded that Kaprian

5

be fired for "kissing her daughter and sexually molesting her." Wimple immediately met with Kaprian and confronted him with the charges. Kaprian denied sexually molesting Barbara but admitted that "in a moment of weakness' he was "overcome by her beauty and kissed her." Wimple was flabbergasted by this explanation, but he chose to take no further action and allowed Kaprian to return to his class. This policy of vacillating and procrastinating came to an end abruptly that afternoon when Mrs. Racklin stormed into the principal's office and demanded to know why "that sex maniac Kaprian" was "still allowed in a classroom with innocent children." She threatened to "summon the police" and to "take legal action unless something was done immediately." A frightened Wimple quickly informed the superintendent's office of the incident, and an appointment was arranged for Mrs. Racklin to see the superintendent the following afternoon. That evening the local newspaper and television station circulated a story about the "kissing math teacher." The issue immediately became a *cause celebre,* and the following morning the superintendent's office was inundated with calls from parents who were angry with the "teacher who violated a student" and concerned over the "safety of their daughters." In her afternoon meeting with the superintendent, Mrs. Racklin reiterated her charges and remained adamant in her insistence that Kaprian be fired. The superintendent, feeling the pressure of public disapproval of the incident and confronted with a strong, articulate parent who could not be pacified, relived Kaprian of all teaching duties and called for an administrative hearing on the charges.

By state law administrative hearings were required for tenured teachers confronted with charges that could result in dismissal. The three administrative officers who conducted the hearing were superintendents of schools from across the state. They were selected as follows: one by both the Board of Education and the superintendent of the school where the incident occurred, a second by the State Commissioner of Education, and the third by the teacher being charged. The officers heard testimony from all parties involved and rendered a decision which was final and not subject to appeal. Their decisions could range from outright dismissal to suspension for various lengths of time to dropping of all charges.

At the hearing, testimony was gathered from Kaprian, Barbara Racklin, Mrs. Racklin, Principal Wimple, and several Trent High School teachers. Kaprian restated that "in the weakness of the moment" he was "overcome by Barbara's beauty and kissed her."

He denied "making any further advances, touching her physically or molesting her in any way." He described his actions as "spontaneous, without motive" and admitted they were "stupid, unnecessary, and regrettable." Barbara Racklin testified that she had "disapproved" and that she had not struggled to free herself because she was "caught by surprise" and he was "very strong." She was uncertain whether he touched her, but she remembered "his heavy chest pressing down on her breasts." Mrs. Racklin expressed fears that her daughter had suffered "severe emotional damage" from the "depravity" of this "hot-pants degenerate." She felt that Kaprian's actions were "unforgivable," that he was a "dirty, lonely, old man suffering a mid-life crisis," and that he should "never be trusted with children again." She "wondered aloud" what else was going on at Trent High School. Principle Wimple expressed "shock and dismay" over what happened. He felt it was an "isolated incident," something "totally unexpected of Kaprian," and certainly something he would "never tolerate" in his school. The faculty were divided in their support of Kaprian. Five of the seven teachers testified that Kaprian was an "excellent, devoted teacher" who "gave fully of himself for the past twenty-one years," and was "liked and respected by the students." They felt he was a "person of high character," who because of "grief and loneliness" had "stumbled this once and behaved foolishly." They felt that he should be required to seek counseling but that he should also be allowed to continue teaching. Two of the teachers testified that Kaprian's conduct was "inexcusable and reflected badly upon all teachers." They felt his actions "confirmed" an earlier, rumored incident in which his "sexual indiscretions endangered the life of a student entrusted to his care."

At the close of the hearing, the administrative officers made a thorough review of the testimony and began the difficult process of arriving at a decision. In their deliberations they were anxious to uphold the school's responsibility for protecting the welfare of its students, but they were also reluctant to dismiss or suspend a respected, competent, twenty-one year veteran teacher unless proper cause had been clearly established. Similarly, they were opposed to any form of sexual indiscretions involving teachers and students, but they were also anxious that any judgment made of such indiscretions must take into consideration any and all factors and extenuating circumstances involved in the incident.

The administrative officers had a difficult decision to make. Should they dismiss Kaprian, thus revoking his tenure and taking away his teaching certificate, or should they take a lesser action rang-ing from outright dismissal of the charges to suspension without pay for a period of three months to three years? What should they do?

# Study Guide for Case #1

To the Instructor and Student:

This guide is designed to assist the student in analyzing this case in the following ways. It suggests:

1. a major *Area of Educational Concern* that is central to the case and upon which the student should focus his/her research efforts.

2. *Concepts* that are related to key dimensions of the case and that the student should seek to understand. These *Concepts* have broad implications for educational theory and practice and are listed as *Pivotal Terms*.

3. *Questions* that are concerned with problems raised by the case and that the student should explore further for possible issues.

4. *Reference Material* that is related to the case and that the student should use as a resource in researching the case.

## Case #1

*"The Kiss"*

1. *Area of Educational Concern:* What constraints should govern all relationships between a teacher and a student?

2. *Concepts-Pivotal Terms:*

| | |
|---|---|
| moral misconduct | accountability |
| teacher certificate | suspension |
| tenure | professional ethics |
| dismissal proceedings | single-parent mother |
| "due process of law" | chaperon |
| role model | role confusion |
| colleague relationships | community image |
| sexual harassment | teacher rights |
| student rights | parent involvement |
| teacher competence | college track program |
| extra curricular activities | faculty morale |
| faculty advisor | classroom management |

3. *Questions:*

Should school policy specify expected standards of behavior between teacher and students?

Who should try teachers in cases involving moral misconduct?

What should be the proper working relationship between teacher and student?

Should principals have tenure?

Should teachers be role models?

Does a teacher's lifestyle influence students' attitudes and preferences?

Should teachers be expected to be guardians of an outmoded code of social behavior?

How much input should lay members of the community have in assessing teacher behavior and performance?

4. *Reference Material:*

Ascik, Thomas R. (1985). The Courts and Education, in Eileen M. Gardner, ed., *A New Agenda for Education.* Washington, DC: The Heritage Foundation.

Blase, Joseph J. (1983). Teachers' perceptions of moral guidance. *The Clearing House,* 56(5), 389–393.

Brandt, Stephen. (1988). On assessment of teaching: A conversation with Lee Shulman. *Educational Leadership,* 46(3), 45.

Firestone William A. (1989). Beyond Order and Expectations in High School. *Education Leadership,* 46(5), 41.

Fisher, Louis. (1973). *The Civil Rights of Teachers.* New York: Harper and Row.

Jackson, Phillip W. (1988). The School as moral instructor. *The World and I,* 3, 593–606.

Martin, M. W. (1989). *Everyday Morality.* Belmont, CA: Wadsworth Publishing Company.

Raths, L., Harmen, M. and S. Simon. (1978). *Values and Teaching.* Columbus, Ohio: Charles E. Merrill.

# Understanding a Friend

Everyone said they should have been brothers. Jeff Reardon and John Reilly were always together sharing each other's victories, defeats, and dreams. They thoroughly enjoyed each other and could always be found together playing, studying, doing chores, and even serving as altar boys at the same mass. Jeff had an older brother, but he was twelve years his senior; and ever since Jeff could remember, he was either studying at the seminary or fulfilling his pastoral duties as a priest. Jeff's father owned a small realty business, and his mother taught in the town's elementary school. Unlike Jeff, John Reilly was an only child. His father was the town police chief, and his mother was a registered nurse at the local hospital.

The town of Hillshire where the two boys grew up had been a small, picturesque New England town with a village green dominated by a white church steeple and with a tree-lined main street graced with elegant Colonial and Victorian homes. But it had gradually developed into a major bedroom community for professional and business people from large neighboring cities. Over the years prior to this growth, Jeff's father had bought up much of the abandoned farmlands on the outskirts of town and when Hillshire became a choice location for housing, his realty business prospered.

Jeff and John attended the local state college, joined the same fraternity, and on occasion double-dated with girls from a neighboring sorority. These years proved particularly difficult and traumatic for John who, after considerable soul searching, realized that while he enjoyed women as friends he was emotionally and sexually drawn to men. John carefully concealed from Jeff the painful inner turmoil he

11

suffered as he struggled to accept his homosexuality. He chose not to reveal his sexual preferences to his friend, fearing that Jeff would not understand.

The two men remained close friends throughout their college years. Jeff earned a degree in Business Administration and also led the college debating team to the regional championship. John earned a degree in math and teacher education; he also was an outstanding player on the varsity football and basketball teams. Both young men were popular on campus. Jeff was persuasive, outgoing, and a leader with organizational skills that insured the success of any campus activity he joined. John had a boyish charm that complimented his rugged good looks and muscular physique. He displayed a quick, perceptive mind in the classroom, was a fierce competitor on the playing field, and enjoyed the respect of his teammates and the admiration of female students. After graduation, Jeff became a partner in his father's realty business and John joined the Peace Corps.

During the next fifteen years, the two friends lost contact with each other as each pursued different careers and adopted totally different lifestyles. Jeff married his high school sweetheart and had four sons. He proved to be an astute businessman, investing his income from the realty business in several profitable commercial ventures that brought new employment opportunities to Hillshire and promoted its overall prosperity. He was viewed as a prominent leader of the business community and was drafted to play an active role in community affairs, serving on various town governance boards and fund-raising committees for charitable organizations.

Jeff found he enjoyed the politics of governing, and his success in this role led him to seek elected public office. He ran for the school committee and, after being elected several terms, became its chairperson. Under his leadership the school committee supported the funding and programs necessary to improve the quality of the Hillshire public school system. Hillshire teachers were paid the highest salaries and fringe benefits in the state, and an elementary school and a high school, equipped with the latest facilities, were built to house the expanding student population. Special committees of administrators and teachers were established to screen all teacher candidates while newly-appointed, tenure-track teachers were regularly observed and evaluated by school administrators and were subject to review and approval by the school committee at the end of each of the three years of their probationary period. Jeff took pride in the improvements his committee had achieved in the school system, but he remained particularly anxious to make the high school, where his children would be soon attending, the finest in the state.

John served two years in the Peace Corps as a math teacher in Africa. He received a special commendation from the host country for his untiring efforts leading to the successful establishment of a program to train math teachers. His dedication to his work was not without its price. He was hospitalized on three different occasions because of amoebic dysentary, malaria, and hepatitis. The experience of working alone in a strange country with a vastly different cultural setting and the weeks spent convalescing in the hospital provided John with ample time and solitude to reflect on the meaning of his sexual preferences, to arrive at an acceptance of himself as a homosexual, and to plan his future around a gay lifestyle.

When John's tour of duty in the Peace Corps ended and he returned to the United States, he took up residence in a gay neighborhood in Wayton, a large city two hundred miles away from Hillshire. He became a math teacher at an inner city public high school located in a ghetto area. He also enrolled at a university in the city, and during evenings, weekends, and summers, he earned a Master's Degree in math and a Certificate of Advanced Graduate Study in computer science and math education. John proved to be an exciting, creative teacher whose course material reflected the most recent developments in the field of math and who used teaching methodologies that were demanding yet responsive to students' needs and interests. John related well to the disadvantaged students. He was firm but fair, demanding but understanding, imposed standards, expected responses, hoped high for them and was willing to meet them half way. In his thirteenth year of teaching, John was selected "Outstanding Teacher of the Year" and received statewide recognition for his exceptional work as an educator. His picture and the story of his award appeared in all the local newspapers.

Jeff learned of his old friend's success in the *Hillshire Journal* and immediately set about renewing his acquaintance with him. Over the next several months John was frequently invited to Jeff's home, and his warm, gracious and charming manner quickly endeared him to the Reardon family. He became "Uncle John" to the four boys with whom he spent seemingly endless hours playing touch football, shooting baskets, talking sports, and recounting tales about childhood adventures he shared with their father.

At the close of the following school year, the chairperson of the math department at the new Hillshire high school retired. Jeff urged his friend to apply for the position, and John was persuaded to do so by the many advantages it offered. Not only would he be playing a key role in curricula development, teaching advanced courses and honors sections to motivated students, having access to a wide array of quality teaching aids, and working in a community where concerned parents valued and supported education, but he would also be receiving a salary with fringe benefits that amounted to a one-hundred percent increase over his present earnings.

John's application was well-received by the screening committee; it nominated him for the position, and the school committee, by a 4 to 1 vote, confirmed his appointment. Jeff strongly endorsed his friend's candidacy and lobbied heavily for committee members to support it unanimously. However, Bill Aimes, who preferred to select from within the math department and promote one of its older members, cast a dissenting vote.

John did not vacate his apartment in Wayton when he assumed his teaching duties in Hillshire. Rather, he rented a small flat in Hillshire and returned to Wayton on weekends and during school holidays. In his first year as chairperson he revamped the curriculum, upgraded course requirements, introduced new texts, expanded computer-based course offerings, and presented workshops to departmental members on the most recent approaches to teaching math. John was heavily committed to all of these changes and pushed hard to implement them. Some faculty members viewed his actions as being "insensitive to the rights of senior department members" and as "callously disregarding established programs that had always been part of the math curriculum." John also served as faculty advisor to the student council and revitalized its role in school affairs by encouraging it to become a sounding board for student concerns about school policy.

In its first annual review of John's performance, the school committee voted 4 to 1 for retention. The high school principal and assistance superintendent submitted a report, based on their observations of John, which praised his effectiveness and commitment. They found him to be a knowledgeable, concerned, and dynamic teacher and administrator who was always available to students, faculty, and parents. Bill Aimes again cast the sole dissenting vote on the school committee. He noted that some members of the math department had complained to him that John was "too pushy and demanding" and that he was making course changes that were "unwise and unnecessary." Another committee member, Andrew Sacor expressed concern that

John, as student council advisor, was encouraging students to question school authority. He was dismayed that his daughter, a member of the student council, had suddenly become a strong advocate of student rights.

In his second year as chairperson, John further polished and refined the changes made in the curriculum. He also organized and trained a math team, and he introduced workshops during after school hours to prepare students for the PSATs and the SATs. John enjoyed widespread praise and support from parents and the administration for his work in the math department; however, his role as student-council advisor involved him in a controversy that raised serious questions among many about his judgment.

As the senior class prepared for its graduation activities, the prom committee was informed by a student that his escort would be a male student. The announcement triggered a storm of controversy in the school and community and resulted in a public outcry in which many parents demanded that the two students be barred from the dance. The school administration, backed by the school committee, directed the students not to attend the dance. One of the students' fathers responded by appealing to the American Civil Liberties Union to intervene and protect his son's rights. In the midst of this turmoil many students asked their student council to address the problem.

In his capacity as advisor, John reminded the council members of their by-laws which required that all dimensions of an issue be examined as part of the decision-making process. He provided them with lists of books, articles, and visual materials that examined the pros and cons of the gay issue from legal, social, religious, historical, and political perspectives. He also assisted them in gaining access to these materials and even obtained much of it for them from a university library in Wayton.

Included in the materials examined by the students were writings that were sympathetic to homosexuality by Don Clark, Andrew Humm, and the Jesuit priest John McNeill, and a Corporation for Public Broadcasting film, *Before Stonewall,* which provided an historical treatment of the gay rights movement based on archival footage. When many of the parents learned the nature of the material to which children on the student council were being exposed, they demanded John be replaced as faculty advisor. Among those most vitriolic in their attack upon John was Andrew Sacor who discovered his daughter reading "that garbage" by Don Clark (*Living Gay*). At the height of all this emotional rhetoric, parental denunciations, and legal threats, the crisis suddenly ended. The parents of the male student who was to be escorted to the dance transferred their son to a private school in another state.

In its second review of John's performance, the school committee voted 3 to 2 for retention. Again, the administration's evaluation of John was highly laudatory noting that his efforts in preparing the math team had been a major factor in their being undefeated in state competition. The evaluation also contained an addendum which noted that John was being relieved of his duties as student council advisor to "allow him more time for the pressing responsibilities of department chairperson." The two dissenting votes on the school committee were cast by Will Aimes and Andrew Sacor. Will Aimes reiterated complaints by math department members concerning John's "leadership style" and his "forcing unneeded curriculum changes." Andrew Sacor made an impassioned speech in which he quoted from the Bible (Romans 1:25–27) and I Cor. 6:9–10) to show that "God is against homosexuality." He concluded by demanding that "this Goddamned queer-loving liberal never be given another opportunity to expose innocent minds to perversion."

John's third year as chairperson passed without incident. He continued to fine tune the changes made in the curriculum, and he initiated a program with the local state college to allow advanced math students to earn college credits during their senior year in courses offered jointly by the college and the high school. The controversy surrounding his role as student-council advisor faded, though the action by Andrew Sacor's daughter and several other students on the student council, who resigned to protest his removal, did not go unnoticed by students and parents.

The weekend prior to the school committee meeting in which John's tenure would be considered, Jeff attended a business conference in Wayton. It was the first time Wayton had been selected for the realtors' convention, and Jeff joined other delegates after meetings ended in exploring the better dining establishments available. On the last evening of the convention, Jeff had dinner at a gay nightclub that was noted for its exceptional cuisine. At the dinner table, Jeff sat next to Megan Fine, a feisty, outspoken, long-time resident of Wayton and an active member of its school committee. The conversation turned to school affairs, and specifically to John Reilly, whom Megan remembered as one of the "best damned teachers we ever had." She regretted that Wayton had not made a greater effort to retain John, and she did not fault him for taking advantage of the Hillshire opportunity. As an afterthought she added, "He's gay, you know; perhaps, he felt Wayton would never trust him with a chairpersonship." At this last statement, all the color drained from Jeff's face. He stared at Megan in disbelief and mumbled something about "not being aware of John's homosexuality." Jeff somehow managed to muddle through the remainder of the evening. He felt John had deceived him, and he was deeply hurt and confused.

Jeff met with John the afternoon before the school committee meeting. He expressed anger and dismay at John's "duplicity" and "failure to admit" he was gay. Jeff felt he should have had such knowledge before deciding to encourage his wife and children to accept John "as family" and before deciding to sponsor and support John's candidacy and career at Hillshire High School. John replied that it took time for him to overcome self-hatred and to accept himself. He said, "Everything in society taught me to hate who I am, and for a time I did! You say I should have told you I was gay. If it took me, with so much at stake, such effort and time to understand, how much more effort and time would be required of you, not being gay and with little at stake, to understand? Would you have found the time or had the inclination to pursue such understanding? I think not! The truth is you prefer not to see me and/or accept me for what I am, and since so much hostility awaits me outside my closet door, I have allowed you and others to presume I am heterosexual and to treat me accordingly." John ended on a poignant note. "Nothing has really changed since last Saturday night. I am still the same person I was before you discovered I was gay. I cherish my friendship with you, love your family as if it were my own, remain committed to applying my professional skills to developing the best educational program possible for Hillshire High School, and enjoy watching my students learn."

That evening the school committee's vote on granting John tenure split 2 to 2 and Jeff had to cast the deciding vote. The administration's evaluation of John praised him for the rich, diverse, and challenging curriculum he had established over the past three years. It applauded the success of his new program allowing students to take courses for college credits, and it noted that Hillshire students had never performed so well on the math sections of the PSATs and SATs. The two dissenting votes on the school committee were again cast by Will Aimes, who repeated faculty complaints about John's "bull in the china shop" type of leadership, and Andrew Sacor, who said he "mirrored the sentiments of many parents" when he continued to express reservations as to whether John's judgment could "ever be fully trusted again."

Jeff had a difficult decision to make. Should he vote to grant tenure and provide John with job security or should he vote to deny tenure and force John to leave Hillshire High School?

Jeff slowly rose to his feet. He realized John's achievements as chairperson and teacher were impressive, but the "bottom line" issue remained: Should a homosexual be allowed to teach the children of Hillshire? How should he vote?

# Study Guide for Case #2

To the Instructor and Student:

This guide is designed to assist the student in analyzing this case in the following ways. It suggests:

1. a major *Area of Educational Concern* that is central to the case and upon which the student should focus his/her research efforts.

2. *Concepts* that are related to key dimensions of the case and that the student should seek to understand. These *Concepts* have broad implications for educational theory and practice and are listed as *Pivotal Terms*.

3. *Questions* that are concerned with problems raised by the case and that the student should explore further for possible issues;

4. *Reference Material* that is related to the case and that the student should use as a resource in researching the case;

## Case #2

*"Understanding a Friend"*

1. *Area of Educational Concern:* Who shall teach our children and by what criteria shall we determine their effectiveness and their acceptability?

2. *Concepts-Pivotal Terms:*

| | |
|---|---|
| accountability | student activities |
| teacher evaluation | local control |
| privacy of family | tenure |
| equal opportunity employment | student civil rights |
| homophobia | Tinker v. DesMoines (1969) |
| Employment Protection Act (1985) | role model |
| self-disclosure ("coming out") | Peace Corps |
| academic freedom | probationary period |
| substantive privacy | nonfeasance |
| malfeasance | historical values |
| normative sexuality | evolving values |

3. *Questions:*

Should an individual's sexual preferences be considered when screening candidates for teaching positions?

Under what conditions should personal friendship preclude official decision making?

Does a teacher have a right to promote public awareness of homosexuality?

To what extent should local community standards and parental preferences shape school programs and policies?

What should be the role of a faculty advisor?

To what extent should teachers have the right to privacy?

Can a teacher's sexual preference affect a child?

Should social questions be decided in absolute terms or by apportionment?

4. *Reference Material:*

Boggan, E. Carrington. (1976). *The Rights of Gay People.* Toronto, Canada: Sunrise Books.

Clark, Don. (1975). *Living gay.* Milbrae, CA: Celestial Arts.

Friends Home Service Committee. (1964). *Towards a Quaker View of Sex.* London, Great Britain: Author.

Hanigan, James P. (1988). *Homosexuality, The Test Case for Christian Sexual Ethics.* New York: The Paulist Press.

Humm, Andrew. (1980). The personal politics of lesbian and gay liberation. *Social Policy,* 11(2), 40–45.

Kozol, Jonathan. (1972). Free schools: A time for candor. *Saturday Review,* 55(10), 51–54.

Palker, Patricia. (1980). Tenure: Do we need it? *Teacher,* 97(8), 36–40.

Schneider-Vogel, Merri. (1986). Gay teachers in the classroom: A continuing constitutional debate. *Journal of Law and Education,* 15(3), 285–318.

Wilson, David E. (1986). Advocating young-adult novels with gay themes. *The Education Digest,* 52(2), 46–49.

# The Prize

Class valedictorian was the singular most coveted honor sought by students graduating from West Langton High School. It was an award paying special tribute to the academic achievement of that one student who outperformed all others by maintaining the highest grade average during the sophomore, junior, and first two semesters of the senior year. Its recipient received public recognition and acclaim at school and community ceremonies, delivered the keynote address at the graduation ceremony, was assured entrance to the more prestigious colleges, and enjoyed increased opportunities for scholarship aid.

There was always fierce competition for this award, and in each graduating class several students became candidates for it by receiving straight A report cards during their sophomore and junior years. However, by the second quarter of the senior year all of these top students, with the exception of one, were eliminated because they were unable to maintain their high grade averages. That one student became the valedictorian and another student, with the second highest average, was awarded the lesser honor of salutatorian.

West Langton High was a comprehensive school with a quality college track program that was filled by the children of college-educated parents who provided professional services to neighboring large cities and to nearby State University. These students were bright, enthusiastic, and highly motivated, and more than eighty percent of them went on to higher education. They enjoyed the challenge of the high school's difficult curriculum, and they found it easy to relate to the faculty, most of whom were life-long residents and had taught their friends, relatives, and other members of their family.

James Lacteau was the newly-appointed principal of West Langton High. He was from out of state and, unlike his predecessors, exercised strong leadership through closer supervision of the faculty and through programs promoting improved school-parent-community relations. During his first year as principal, he visited classrooms, talked with students and teachers, and met with parents. While he was favorably impressed with much of what he observed and heard, he also had serious reservations about the policies and practices of several of the faculty. He was particularly concerned with those of Ruth Becker, the chairperson of the math department who taught most of the courses in the honors program. In his meetings with honors students and their parents, he sensed a general undercurrent of discontent directed at Becker's testing and grading policy and her approach to parent-teacher conferences. Students were passing the course but seemed resigned to testing and grading practices they neither understood nor felt were fair. Parents seemed frustrated by Becker's willingness to meet with them but her failure to address the concerns they raised.

At the close of the school year, Lacteau attempted to discuss these negative impressions with Becker, but she became highly defensive. She dismissed any suggestions of discontent as "sour grapes by slow students" unable to meet the demands of an accelerated honors math course and as "whining by pushy parents" disappointed in their efforts to pressure her to raise their child's grade. She noted that in her twenty-one years of teaching, no principal had ever questioned her teaching ability, and she reminded him that the union contract carefully spelled out legal proceedings that must be followed if a tenured teacher's competence were to be questioned. She concluded by suggesting that he "trust and support" his teachers rather than "chase rumors and harass them." Lacteau was disturbed by Becker's response and attitude but chose not to pursue the issue further at that time.

The following fall term the chairperson of the history department suffered a serious heart attack two weeks after classes started. Charlie Fong, a Ph.D. candidate in history, was hired as a long-term substitute. Fong had been a high school history teacher for several years in a neighboring large city before he entered the doctoral program at State University. He was paying for his graduate education by doing substitute teaching, and West Langton had hired him on several previous occasions. He was an excellent teacher with a rich background in his subject matter area; therefore, he had little difficulty assuming the chairperson's teaching load which included an eleventh grade honors course in American History.

On the first day of teaching, Fong sat next to Ruth Becker during lunch. In the course of their conversation, she commented that he had "both contenders for the prize" in his honors history class. When Fong seemed puzzled by her remark, she explained that he would be teaching Len Becker and Craig Rolli; they were the only straight A students left in the junior class and, therefore, remained the "most likely candidates for the prize of class valedictorian." She was confident that as each marking period passed and the pressure to continue to excel increased, the "lesser student would falter" and only the "most qualified" would remain "to claim the prize." She then added, with a slight smile on her lips, "Let's see who stumbles first."

Fong was astonished by Becker's comments which he felt revealed her undue concern and involvement in, and her careful monitoring of, a student award that he had always assumed was determined in an impartial way free of teacher manipulation. He now became curious about these two students and began to observe them closely in his class. He found them to be bright, but dramatically different, in their application of intellectual and social skills and in their personalities and conception of self. Len Becker was the nephew of Ruth Becker. He had good study habits, was always prepared for class recitations, and was able to repeat in detail large quantities of material taken from lectures and readings. His treatment of material was descriptive and void of any analytical, speculative or interpretive comments. He was a tall, handsome youth with a friendly, outgoing personality that made him popular with faculty and classmates. He exuded confidence and was a master at projecting a surface image of the "good guy:" always charming, pleasant, affable, concerned.

Craig Rolli was the second of three sons of Dominic Rolli, the night editor of a major newspaper in a large neighboring city. Craig was a voracious reader, with an insatiable thirst for knowledge, and an unbounding curiosity. He grasped concepts quickly, asked penetrating questions, offered provocative and creative interpretations, and displayed high levels of critical thinking and analytical skills in his approach to the various subject matter areas. He was a slender youth of average looks and height, with hunched shoulders, and thick-lens glasses that hung half-way down his nose. He was quiet, withdrawn, lacked the social skills to cultivate friends and the confidence and poise to ingratiate himself with teachers. Students viewed him as a "study nut" and "somewhat of a nerd," while teachers marveled at his intelligence but were dismayed by his social naivete.

Fong enjoyed teaching both students and found their input into class discussions invaluable. He was particularly drawn to Craig whose questions and comments revealed a love and understanding of history very similar to his own. He often enjoyed after school discussions with him in which they further explored issues raised in class or exchanged views on books they had read. A close friendship developed, and Craig confided in Fong, revealing to him the suffering of a lonely, unhappy, tortured youth, anxious to make friends and be accepted by others but shackled by lack of confidence and fear of rejection. Craig sought to compensate for his feelings of social inadequacy by excelling as a student. He confessed to Fong that it was only through his academic successes and achievements that his "sense of personal worth" was enhanced and he enjoyed "recognition and acceptance by others." To become class valedictorian was more than just the consolation prize, it was critical to his *raison d'etre.*

On the day prior to the end of the first quarter marking period, several teachers in the faculty room at lunch time were admiring poems submitted by Craig Rolli as part of his honors English project. The chairperson of the English department was so impressed by them, she had taken the opportunity to share them with her colleagues. In the middle of the chorus of praise for Craig, Ruth Becker suddenly turned to Fong and asked how the "contenders for the prize" had fared in his course. Fong said both were "excellent students" and had received A. As he finished speaking, Becker slowly shook her head and said, "This has not been the case in Math. One of the contenders has stumbled."

The following morning grade reports were issued, and that afternoon a solemn and dejected Craig Rolli sat through Fong's class without uttering a word. After class, Craig told Fong he received a C-in Ruth Becker's honors math course. This low grade made it "impossible" for him to earn higher than a B+ cumulative grade in math for the year, and it "virtually destroyed" his chances of becoming valedictorian. Fong suggested that the "prize isn't important but rather how you play the game." Craig's eyes glistened as he fought back tears and his voice rose in anger. "You don't understand," he said, "whatever I do cannot affect the outcome. How well I perform has nothing to do with the grade I receive. Only Miss Becker's grading practices determine who wins and who loses." He then explained three of these practices and showed how they determined his grade.

First, weightings and allotted time for each test item were not listed on exams, but were assigned by Ruth Becker as she corrected tests. Since exams contained more test items than could be answered in the allotted time, students had to guess at which questions to devote more or less time on and which ones to skip. Craig Rolli did well on all test items he answered, but they were not the items Ruth Becker decided to assign the most credit to when she graded the papers. Second, Ruth Becker did not return corrected exams until weeks after they were taken, and students were allowed to view them only briefly in class before returning them to her. If students had questions regarding corrections, they were to be noted on the corrected exams for her consideration. However, once exams were returned to Ruth Becker, students never saw them again and rarely received a reply to their questions. When Craig Rolli persisted on receiving an explanation for Ruth Becker's corrections on one of his exams, she ridiculed him before the class calling him a "grade-grubber". Finally, Ruth Becker used seven tests taken over a period of nine weeks as the basis for quarterly grades; however, she never informed students as to the worth of each test in determining this grade. When Craig Rolli questioned his quarterly grade of C-, noting that five of his seven test grades had been A, Ruth Becker explained that he had performed well on the tests of least value.

Fong knew that Craig was a victim of poor teaching practices and, perhaps, even of Becker's favoritism for her nephew. But he realized that little could be done to correct the situation because Becker was an established, tenured teacher whose competence could not be easily challenged. He sought instead to encourage Craig by agreeing that "Becker's teaching practices were poor" but urging him to "rise above them and do his very best regardless of the outcome." He reminded Craig of the Yogi Berra aphorism, "It ain't over till its over." Then he added, almost as an afterthought, "the leading candidate could also stumble, and you again would have an equal chance for the prize."

Dominic Rolli was disappointed with his son's low math grade, and he sought to monitor Craig's performance during the second quarter of the school year. When Ruth Becker failed to return any corrected exams after six weeks of classes, he requested a conference with Principal Lacteau and Ruth Becker. Becker brought to the conference a pile of corrected exams with A grades to show that most of her students understood the material and performed well on the exams. Dominic Rolli was allowed to view his son's exam, but Becker refused to discuss her grading practices. When he persisted in his questioning and received no satisfactory response, he condemned her grading policies as "arbitrary, capricious, and totally without rationale" and stormed out of the meeting.

Two days later the local newspaper carried a lengthy guest editorial by Dominic Rolli entitled "Teachers and Their Games." The author suggested that teachers who "cannot effectively deal with ideas or students" survive in the profession because they develop classroom procedures that shield their incompetency and "reduce the act of teaching to a form of game." While the author did not name any specific teacher as being incompetent and only briefly listed types of games and the malpractices they reflected, he did describe in detail an "insidious and vicious game" that masked grading practices similar to those of Ruth Becker. He attacked this game for "creating an environment of fear and intimidation by not informing students as to how they would be evaluated" and for "promoting anxiety and frustration by delaying the return of corrected materials." The editorial concluded with an eloquent plea for the "removal of incompetent teachers" and an "end to the games they play."

The Rolli editorial caused an uproar in the school. Len Barker collected student signature on a petition denouncing the editorial as an "unwarranted attack on the teaching profession" and as a "veiled attempt to impugn the reputation of an excellent teacher." Fong and several other teachers refused to have the petition circulated during class time, and they also complained to Principal Lacteau that the petition was "proving disruptive and divisive." Another group of teachers led by Ruth Becker interrupted class lessons to insure students signed the petition. These teachers also ignored student heckling of Craig Rolli during class time until Ruth Becker's math class was disrupted by a fist fight between Rolli and one of Len Becker's followers.

News of this scuffle led Principal Lacteau to stop the circulation of the petition on school time and to confront Ruth Becker on her teaching practices. In a meeting held shortly before the end of the second quarter, he expressed his discontent with her "questionable" grading practices, her "failure to address parental concerns" at conferences held with them, and her failure to "curb the highly provocative behavior of certain students" that had resulted in the scuffle during her class. A heated exchange followed in which Ruth Becker again reminded the principal of her tenured status and her rights under the union contract. Lacteau acknowledged that her "tenured status and the teachers' union defending it'' presented "formidable obstacles" to challenging her competency in the courts. However, there were certain "administrative actions" he could take to "promote and protect the welfare of all the students." He then handed her a written directive he had prepared prior to their meeting. It ordered the following. First, at the close of the second quarter, Craig Rolli was to be transferred to an honors math class taught by another teacher. Second, under no circumstances was Ruth Becker to teach any twelfth grade honor sections the following year. Third, Lacteau was to be present at all future parent-teacher conferences held by Ruth Becker. And fourth, Ruth Becker must conform to school policies regarding grading practices (specific listing of item weightings, returning of exams, etc.) that would be developed during the third quarter by a special committee of faculty appointed and headed by Lacteau.

Lacteau's actions quickly defused the controversy and disruption that had gripped the school, and the last half of the school year passed uneventfully. Though Ruth Becker assigned Craig Rolli another C- in honors math for the second quarter, he earned straight A grade reports for the remaining quarters and brought his cumulative math grade for the third year to a B-. Thus, at the end of the school year, Len Becker led the junior class with A grades in all subjects, and Craig Rolli ranked second with A grades in all subjects save a B- in honors math.

On the last week of school, Lacteau approached Fong on his availability for the following year if the ailing chairperson of the history department were unable to return. Fong was anxious to resume his doctoral studies full time but agreed to teach the first two quarters if asked. It was also decided that Fong could change the senior honors history course, which would be part of his teaching load, to include assignments requiring more critical, analytical, and interpretive thinking.

The following September Fong returned when the ailing chairperson was unable to resume teaching. He immediately changed the format of the honors history course and required a term paper and two one-hour essay exams, each worth one-third of the total grade. Each essay consisted of two quotes by famous men of the historical period being examined. Students were to select one of the quotes and to identify its author, place it within its historical context, interpret the ideology and/or social, economic, and political factors it reflected, and explain its significance for the period/nation/etc. involved. The

27

term paper followed a similar format only the student provided the quote used. Fong devoted considerable time and effort during the initial classes to prepare the students for analyzing quotes, and his efforts were rewarded by the excellent term papers they submitted after the first five weeks of the quarter. Most of the students received B or better, and both Craig Rolli and Len Becker received A. Students again performed well two weeks later on the first essay exam, but while Craig Rolli maintained an A, Len Becker had considerable difficulty analyzing the quote and fell to a B. In a meeting with Fong, he expressed disappointment and annoyance, but he did not dispute the grade after Fong had him read the A essays written by his classmates. On the final essay exam, Craig Rolli easily earned an A, but Len Becker continued to have difficulty and his grade fell to a C. Consequently, his quarterly grade in honors history averaged B, and for the first time, he failed to earn a straight A report.

During the first weeks of the following quarter Len Becker remained after school each day and sought additional assistance from Fong. At first he seemed to be responding to this extra help as he matched Craig Rolli's A on the term paper due the fifth week of the quarter. But two weeks later, he had difficulty with the essay exam and received C while many of his classmates, including Craig Rolli, received A. On the day exams were returned, Fong was confronted after class by a concerned Len Becker who complained that he had "never had this problem with a course before" and that it "almost seemed" he was "destined to receive a low grade." Becker's face became ashen and his voice strained as he spoke of the importance of becoming class valedictorian. It would "insure him early admission to a prestigious college," and he would "become eligible for a large scholarship" from his father's place of employment. As Becker spoke, he became highly emotional: his lips quivered and his voice cracked. "Please, Mr. Fong," he begged, "I need at least a B on the final essay. Without it my cumulative grade in honors history will fall below B, and I will no longer have the highest grade average in the senior class. My only chance to become class valedictorian will be gone. Everything hangs on this exam and how you grade it!"

The following afternoon, several teachers led by Ruth Becker met with Principal Lacteau. They had learned of Len Becker's difficulties in the honors history class, and they expressed reservations about Fong and how the class was being taught. They were concerned that an "outsider," a substitute teacher who was not a regular member of the teaching staff, should have "such critical input" in the determination of the highest honor West Langton bestowed on one of its students. They also questioned his changes in the format of the honors history course and his "experimenting" with a teaching approach that "belonged more in college than in high school." Lacteau listened politely, but he quickly dismissed their complaints by reminding them that Fong was a "state certified teacher officially appointed by the town of West Langton" and in this capacity he would receive the "full backing of the principal's office to carry out his assigned professional duties and responsibilities."

On the day of the honors history exam, Len Becker complained that he needed extra time to complete his essay. Though Fong required that exams be completed within the allotted time, he realized the importance of this exam to the student, and he allowed him an extra twenty-five minutes. Fong corrected the exams that evening and found that most of the students maintained grades of B or better and that Craig Rolli easily earned an A. However, Fong had considerable difficulty grading Len Becker's exam. It was several pages longer than any of the others, did not seem to focus on the quote given, and developed a statement, explanation, and interpretation of the quote that was highly ambiguous. After rereading the exam several times, Fong realized that the essay could be graded either B or D depending on how the reader chose to view it.

The next morning Fong asked the other four teachers in the history department to read the exam and grade it. Two of the teachers assigned it a B, and the other two assigned it a D. Before leaving school that afternoon, Fong met with Principal Lacteau and explained the dilemma created by Len Becker's exam. Lacteau unequivocally affirmed his support for whatever decision Fong made. He admitted that he was "glad" it was not his decision to make because his confrontations with Ruth Becker had destroyed his objectivity. Then he added, "I am confident that whatever decision you make will be based on Len Becker's performance on the exam and on nothing more!"

That evening Fong completed grading the final exams. When he came to Len Becker's exam, he read it through again and reflected on the difficult decision confronting him. He realized how much the class valedictorian award meant to both Craig Rolli and Len Becker: for the former, it had become his *raison d'etre,* absolutely identified with his sense of personal worth; for the latter it had become a critical ingredient in his future educational plans. Fong was also painfully aware that he must not allow his decision to be prejudiced by his admiration of and compassion for Craig Rolli and by his general dislike of Len Becker and his abhorrence of his aunt's malicious efforts to manipulate the selection of class valedictorian.

Fong had a difficult decision to make. If he assigned a B to the exam, Len Becker would retain the highest grade average in the senior class and would be awarded class valedictorian. If he assigned a D to the exam, Craig Rolli's grade average would become the highest in the senior class, and he would be awarded class valedictorian. What should he do?

# Study Guide for Case #3

To the Instructor and Student:

This guide is designed to assist the student in analyzing this case in the following ways. It suggests:

1. a major *Area of Educational Concern* that is central to the case and upon which the student should focus his/her research efforts.

2. *Concepts* that are related to key dimensions of the case and that the student should seek to understand. These *Concepts* have broad implications for educational theory and practice and are listed as *Pivotal Terms.*

3. *Questions* that are concerned with problems raised by the case and that the student should explore further for possible issues;

4. *Reference Material* that is related to the case and that the student should use as a resource in researching the case;

## Case #3
### *"The Prize"*

1. *Area of Educational Concern:* Can a school develop a policy for conferring honors on its students that is free of manipulation and "politics"?

2. *Concepts-Pivotal Terms:*

| | |
|---|---|
| class valedictorian | essay exam |
| critical thinking | conception of self |
| substitute teacher | professional ethics |
| analytical skills | nepotism |
| tenure | parent-teacher conference |
| teacher evaluation | state certified teacher |
| union contract | nonfeasance of duty |
| grading practices | malfeasance of duty |
| insubordination | honors class |
| competition | class participation |
| cumulative grade average | teacher competence |
| college track program | student rights |

3. *Questions:*

Should students/parents/administrators provide input on the development of teacher grading practices?

Should a school confer honors on its students?

Is tenure an obstacle to change and reform in teaching practices?

Should teachers have their children/relatives as students in school?

Should teachers be allowed to form/join unions?

Is competition in the classroom healthy or counterproductive?

Do tenure laws protect incompetent teachers?

What should be the role of a department chairperson?

What objectives/criteria should guide teachers in test construction and in grading.

4. *Reference Material:*

Blase, Joseph J. (1983). Teachers' perceptions of moral guideance. *The Clearing House,* 56(5), 389–393.

Emmers, Amy Puett. (1981). *After The Lesson Plan.* New York: Teachers College Press.

Heavilin, Barbara Anne. (1986). Confusion confounded: Incompetence among public school teachers. *The Teacher Educator,* 22(2), 19–28.

Lieberman, Myron. (1986). *Beyond Public Education.* New York: Praeger Publishers.

Postman, Neil. (1979). *Teaching As A Conserving Activity.* New York: Delacorte Press.

Sewall, Gilbert T. (1983). *Necessary Lessons.* New York: The Free Press.

Smith, D. K. (1977). Teacher styles of the classroom management. *Journal of Educational Research,* 71(5), 277–282.

Strenio, Andrew J. (1981). *The Testing Trap.* London: Rawson, Wade Publishers.

# A Question of Accountability

Few would dispute it. When Maureen Casey joined the English department at Old English High, she was the most beautiful teacher on the faculty. At twenty-one years of age, this former campus beauty queen, had golden blond hair, blue eyes, a turned-up nose, pearly white teeth and a striking figure. Female students sought to emulate her disarming smile, charming manners, gracious walk, and stylish dress, while male students enjoyed her sincerity and friendliness and secretly nurtured "schoolboy crushes." Several of the faculty members had dated her, and Jim O'Neill, the guidance teacher, had seriously courted her.

Maureen Casey was the oldest daughter of a first generation Irish family that had settled in the large industrial city of Towell. Her father and mother had worked long hours in a textile mill and had made considerable sacrifices to educate both their children. Maureen's older brother became a lawyer, and she was sent to one of the finest private colleges in the area. Shortly after she graduated, her father suffered a critical heart attack and passed away. Since her older brother had married and had moved across country, Maureen remained at home with her mother and took a teaching position at Old English High.

Old English was one of the better high schools in the region. Most of its students went on to college, and its alumni occupied the leading professional positions in Towell. Maureen taught Shakespeare, creative writing, and poetry, and she served as faculty advisor to the school's literary periodical—a publication which won several state and regional awards for the quality of its articles. Students found her to be a demanding but fair teacher who knew her subject matter and enjoyed teaching it. She was well-organized, corrected and returned papers promptly, and expected her students to complete assignments on time and be prepared to participate in class discussions.

During her first five years of teaching, Maureen dated Jim O'Neill frequently but refused to consider marriage because of her deep feelings of responsibility to her mother. Eventually the relationship broke off, and Jim married someone else. Other suitors followed in Jim's path with similar results, and by her fortieth birthday Maureen found herself loved by her students, respected by her colleagues, and courted by no one. Her entire life focused upon taking care of her widowed mother and teaching.

The city of Towell had grown and changed during the first twenty years of Maureen's teaching career. As the population expanded, there was a migration of the professional and middle class from the older commercial and industrial southern area of the city, where old English was located, to the undeveloped and rural northern area. To accommodate this population shift, a new high school was built in the area, and the children of the professional and middle class families transferred out of Old English to attend it. Their places were filled by children from the inner core of the city, and for the first time in its history the faculty at Old English found itself wrestling with the problems of teaching the disadvantaged. The effects upon the curriculum were dramatic. The college preparatory program was sharply curtailed, and commercial, vocational, and general courses predominated.

Maureen found few students interested in her courses in Shakespeare, creative writing, and poetry, and she was forced to replace them with offerings in business English and in general literature that made only brief references to Shakespeare and poetry. She lost her role as advisor to the literary periodical which was discontinued for lack of publishable material. She continued to demand quality work from her students, but her efforts were frustrated by classes made up mostly of students who had been socially promoted, who were from socially and economically disadvantaged backgrounds, and who planned to drop out of school on their sixteenth birthday.

In the spring of her thirty-first year of teaching, Maureen's mother died. Maureen suddenly felt as if her world had come to an end: she was growing old; she had not married; she found teaching to be exhausting, frustrating, and increasingly less rewarding because of the type of courses she was forced to offer and the quality of students in her classes; she had lost the only close companion she had shared her life with over the years. Maureen became severely depressed, suffered an emotional breakdown, and was institutionalized. Jim O'Neill, who had recently been appointed superintendent of schools, granted her a sick leave with pay for one year.

The following September Maureen resumed her teaching duties, and during the next five years faculty members noticed an appreciable change in her dress and behavior. She wore crinolines to hide her heavy set body and garish clothing that matched her thick makeup. Young male faculty and older male students found her to be aggressively flirtatious and were annoyed and embarrassed by her batting eyelashes, pawing hands, and suggestive remarks. Maureen's approach to teaching also changed. While she still insisted that students complete assignments, she never failed a student, and, it was rumored, rarely returned corrected papers and tests. Her classes were frequently noisy, but she never indicated any problems existed by sending students to the vice principal's office to be disciplined.

In the summer following her thirty-sixth year of teaching, Old English was refurbished. The workmen painting Maureen's room discovered cabinets full of uncorrected students' papers that dated five years back. When Superintendent O'Neill was informed of this, he directed the principal to say nothing and to observe Maureen's classes closely during the coming year. After several weeks of school in the fall, the principal reported that Maureen's lessons appeared to be poorly organized and offered little material of substance, that her students tended to be so unruly he sometimes feared for her very safety, and that he never saw her return any corrected tests, papers, and assignments.

The following week Superintendent O'Neill held a conference with Maureen. He began by praising her past teaching excellence and her unselfish devotion to her students during her long and distinguished career. He expressed his regret over the changes that Old English had suffered both in the quality of curricula offered and type of student attending. He suggested that she had found it difficult to adjust to these changes and that, unfortunately, she had engaged in practices over the past five years that had seriously undermined her effectiveness as a teacher. He noted that she had given fully and freely of herself over the years and that she should not be expected to sacrifice even further by struggling with the problems currently plaguing Old English. He concluded by recommending that she retire at the end of the school year and by warning her that the questions raised concerning her competency in recent years could provide grounds for her dismissal. When he finished speaking, Maureen said nothing and left the office.

Three days later Superintendent O'Neill received a registered letter from Maureen's lawyer. It stated the following: that teaching was an important part of his client's life as well as being essential to her livelihood; that his client would not consider retiring until she was sixty when she would be eligible for a full pension or, perhaps, not until the mandatory retirement age of seventy; that if the Superintendent was suggesting that his client be relieved of her teaching duties on the grounds of incompetency or whatever, then the law (due process clause) required she be confronted with the charges and be given a hearing. Copies of the letter were sent to the state commissioner of education and to the counsel for the teachers' union.

Before acting on the letter, Superintendent O'Neill asked for written opinions from the school department's lawyer, the principal of Old English, and the English department chairperson of Old English. From the lawyer he learned that under the requirements of due process a hearing would require testimony of witnesses and the submission of materials (reports, evaluations, etc.) that would clearly establish the incompetency of the teacher. The lawyer felt that the former would be difficult to attain because most teachers are hesitant to testify against the practices of a member of their own profession. Similarly, the latter would be difficult to attain because the administration had never compiled written periodical evaluations and reports on the teacher involved.

From the principal he learned that the faculty was divided in their opinion of Maureen as a teacher. Most of the older teachers were sympathetic toward her. They remembered her as an unselfish, conscientious, and dedicated teacher who had devoted more than half her life to the classroom, and they felt it would be cruel to try her as an incompetent in the twilight of her career. They also questioned how much damage she was doing to the students in her classes. They pointed out that until the uncorrected papers were discovered, no one—teacher, pupil, parent, or administrator—had complained about the competency of Maureen as a teacher or about the quality of education in her classes. Further, they felt Maureen was a "burnout victim" of the administration's failure to retrain the older faculty at Old English so that it could understand and meet the needs of the disadvantaged students. Most of the younger teachers took the opposite position. They felt Maureen was not qualified to teach because she suffered from an emotional illness caused by problems of a personal nature that were totally unrelated to her teaching. They were convinced that any attempt to retrain her would prove futile because she was fixed in her traditional, conservative, classical approach to teaching and the curriculum. Finally, they remained highly critical of "older faculty blinded by sentimentalism" who would excuse Maureen's present incompetency on the grounds that she had been an excellent teacher years ago. They argued for her dismissal and urged that she be replaced by a younger teacher with special training in working with the disadvantaged.

From the chairperson of the English department, he learned that students never complained about Maureen's teaching. While the chairperson admitted he had not visited her classes that frequently, he felt that they were no more noisier or disorganized than that of some of the younger teachers in his department. He said he was unhappy to learn that Maureen had not returned corrected tests and papers, but he noted that despite her failure to do so she had developed grades for all her students and was never challenged on them.

Superintendent O'Neill carefully studied each opinion. He felt the school system had certain obligations to a teacher who had given so much of her self for so many years, but he also recognized the school system's responsibility to provide all students with the best education possible. He was not anxious to become involved in the controversy and legal battle that would accompany charges of incompetency; yet, he was genuinely concerned about the educational welfare of the children in Maureen's classes. What should he do? Should he dismiss Maureen or should he allow her to continue to teach?

# Study Guide for Case #4

To the Instructor and Student:

This guide is designed to assist the student in analyzing this case in the following ways. It suggests:

1. a major *Area of Educational Concern* that is central to the case and upon which the student should focus his/her research efforts.

2. *Concepts* that are related to key dimensions of the case and that the student should seek to understand. These *Concepts* have broad implications for educational theory and practice and are listed as *Pivotal Terms.*

3. *Questions* that are concerned with problems raised by the case and that the student should explore further for possible issues;

4. *Reference Material* that is related to the case and that the student should use as a resource in researching the case;

## Case #4

*"A Question of Accountability"*

1. *Area of Educational Concern:* How does a school system respond to the problems created by forces beyond its control (emotional illness of staff; disadvantaged students reflecting populations shifts, economic, and social change) that have an immediate bearing on curriculum, teacher competency, and student performance?

2. *Concepts-Pivotal Terms:*

| | |
|---|---|
| disadvantaged students | burnout |
| social mobility | inner city school |
| tenure | due process clause |
| conservative/classical curriculum | evaluation/grading |
| accountability | teacher competency |
| edumetric testing | grade inflation |
| sexual harassment | sick leave |
| teacher union | social promotion |

| classroom management | dismissal |
| mandatory retirement age | retraining teachers |

3. *Questions:*

Should the curriculum for the disadvantaged be different from that for other students?

Should teachers be evaluated frequently, and if so, by whom?

Should teachers of disadvantaged students be trained differently from those who teach other students?

Should there be job security, through tenure laws or the due process clause, for teachers?

What responsibility does a school system have to the competent teacher who, after years of service, suffers burnout or an emotional illness?

How can schools help teachers to cope with stressful classroom situations?

Are student ratings an effective tool in measuring teaching competence?

4. *Reference Material:*

Bridges, Edwin M. (1986). *The Incompetent Teacher*. Philadelphia, PA: Falmer Press.

Farber, Barry A. and Miller, Julie. (1981). Teacher burnout: A psychoeducational perspective. *Teachers College Record,* 83(2), 235–243.

Lieberman, Myron. (1980). Tenure: Do we need it? *Teacher,* 97(8), 36–40.

Palker, Patricia. (1986). *Beyond Public Education.* New York: Praeger.

Riesman, David. (1954). Teachers amid changing expectations. *Harvard Educational Review,* 24(2), 106–117.

Rodin, Miriam. (1975). Rating the teacher. *Education Digest,* 41(3), 54–57.

Schug, Mark C. (1983). Teacher burnout and professionalism. *Issues In Education,* 1(2 and 3), 133–153.

Sparks, Dennis. (1979). A teacher center tackles the issue. *Today's Education,* 68(4), 37–39.

Van Cleve Morris et al. (1984). *Principals in Action.* Columbus, OH: Charles E. Merrill.

# Between Heaven and Hell

It had been a difficult decision! Dr. Hank Terry had serious reservations when he accepted the post of Assistant Superintendent of the Coalton School District. He realized that he "owed his appointment" to Michael Sloan, the President of the Board of Education and the singular most powerful figure in the district. He was certain that he had been selected by Sloan from among the five finalists only because he lacked experience, and his responses to interview questions concerning racial issues had been ambivalent and noncommittal. He also realized that Coalton's all-white Board of Education had been patently ignoring a festering racial crisis fueled by the Board's failure to desegregate its schools and to recruit blacks for teacher and administrative positions. Yet despite these concerns, Terry had taken the position because it paid well, offered the challenges and experiences of a large, cosmopolitan, prestigious, school district and contrasted sharply with the low-paying, routine administrative post he had held in a small, rural midwestern school system.

Coalton School District, which contained five elementary schools, a middle school, and a high school encompassed the City of Coalton and several highly-affluent neighboring communities (Fig. 5.1). It was boarded on the north by a sparsely-populated, mountainous and forested region and on the south by a major inland waterway. A major landmark on the northern boundary was the beautiful St. Mark's Roman Catholic Seminary with its majestic buildings and splendidly landscaped grounds. A major landmark on the southern boundary was the aging state prison with its massive gray walls and ugly barren grounds surrounded by a high fence. Of Coalton School

41

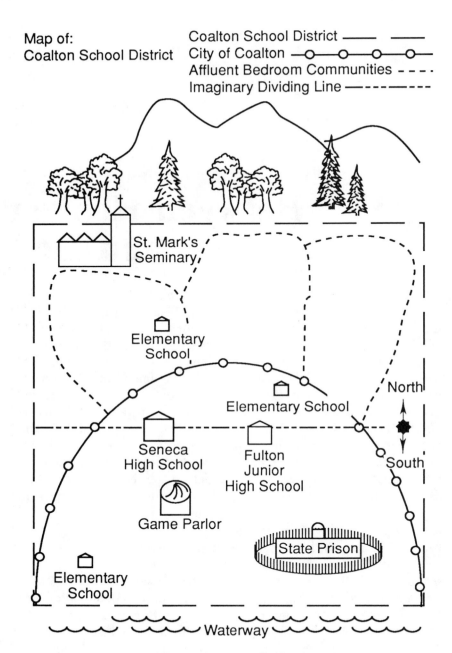

**Map of:**
**Coalton School District**

Coalton School District ⎯ ⎯
City of Coalton ⎯o⎯o⎯o⎯o⎯
Affluent Bedroom Communities - - - -
Imaginary Dividing Line ⎯ - - - ⎯ - -

St. Mark's
Seminary

Elementary
School

Elementary School

North

Seneca
High School

Fulton
Junior
High School

South

Game Parlor

State Prison

Elementary
School

Waterway

**Figure 5.1.** Map of Coalton School District

District's seventy-five thousand residents, seventy-five percent were white and twenty-five percent were black. Most of the affluent whites resided in expensive, spacious homes in the northern half of the district while most of the poor blacks lived in deteriorating ghettos in the southern half. The population mix in the schools paralleled this division with ninety-eight percent of the student body white in the northern elementary schools and fifty-five percent black in the southern ones.

The bulk of the area comprising the school district centered around the City of Coalton where Fulton Junior High School and Seneca Senior High School were located. Coalton was a sprawling city marked by a unique blending of old and new industrial and residential developments. Newly-constructed residential and office complexes of national conglomerates were randomly scattered among decaying smokestack industries while clusters of high-priced suburban dwellings, shielded by groves of trees, were located a short distance from inner city slums. The high school's student body closely reflected this sharply contrasting social and economic structure of the city and district. Seneca High School straddled the imaginary line that could be drawn to divide the white, affluent, and well-educated residents of the district from those who were black, poor, and unskilled. Twenty-five percent of its sixteen hundred students came from the low-income black families who worked in the old industrial plants. The remaining seventy-five percent came from the high-income, mostly white families of the original residents of the district and of the recently-arrived professionals who worked in the research and office complexes.

But while Seneca High School's student body epitomized the polarized socio-economic class structure dividing the district, its faculty, programs, and policies remained totally oblivious and indifferent to the potential racial conflict this structure could produce. Only two of Seneca's seventy-five faculty members were black, and most of the white teachers were life-long residents of Coalton who harbored local prejudices against "those lazy, ignorant, poor blacks." Consequently, Seneca's curriculum, guidance program, school-sponsored social activities, and general policies governing the school program lacked input from professional representatives and lay members of the black community and remained insensitive to the needs and demands of this large minority segment of its population. When several incidents occurred involving racial slurs by teachers, altercations between black and white students, and parental accusations of discriminatory school practices, their significance was belittled by Seneca's principal who dismissed them as "unfortunate," "isolated," "atypical," and "misunderstandings by a few extremists or hotheads."

At the time Hank Terry assumed his duties, he found the superintendent's office stonewalling efforts by the black community, which was supported by the local NAACP and the ACLU, to force the school district to end *de facto* segregation in the elementary schools, to engage in the active recruitment of black personnel, and to develop programs responsive to black students' needs. The superintendent, Stuart Carns, planned to retire in two years; therefore, he sought to contain and avoid acting upon these potentially explosive racial issues, delaying their inevitable consequences until after he left office. To give the appearance he was responding to black demands, without committing himself to any specific substantive changes, he directed Terry to undertake a year-long study of the school system with the objective of recommending programs that would "promote racial harmony within the schools and between the schools and the community." Terry was to report his findings and recommendations on September 1st of the following year.

Throughout the school year, Terry examined programs, observed classes, interviewed teachers and administrators, and talked to students and parents. He found dramatic differences between the all-white elementary schools in the northern area of the school district and those with black majorities in the southern area. Teacher morale, student performance, academic programs, and school facilities were far superior in the former where a school ethos focusing upon a love of, and desire to, learn were produced by well-prepared teachers with high expectations who made effective use of classroom time. In contrast, school facilities in the southern area suffered from extensive vandalism and were characterized by discipline problems, watered-down curriculum, and poorly-prepared teachers who held low expectations that translated into a self-fulfilling prophecy of accepting low pupil performances.

Terry found this self-fulfilling prophecy operating on the secondary level as well. The all-white guidance department at Seneca High School tended to place black students in the vocational and general programs and to encourage white students to take college preparatory or commercial programs. Most white teachers displayed little understanding or patience with classes in the non-college track courses that were filled with culturally disadvantaged black students. They taught little substantive material, expected less from the students, and socially promoted anyone who did not prove disruptive in class. They viewed these students as the "dregs of society," felt that they "did not belong in school," and complained that the school was "expected to succeed where parents had failed." For these white teachers, blacks, with few exceptions were suspect; they "lacked ambition," displayed "little academic ability," and seemed to "excel only on the athletic field."

While Terry discovered racial stereotyping and various expressions of prejudice to be common among many of the white faculty at Seneca High, he also found a small number of white teachers who believed in the black students, hoped high for them, demanded responses from them, and were willing to meet them half way. These teachers offered exciting, challenging courses and were instrumental in channeling several black students each year into college track programs. Among these teachers was Gerald Fishbein, a talented, creative English teacher who was respected by faculty, students, and parents for his integrity, objectivity, and fairness. He had formerly taught in an inner city school and had extensive experience working with disadvantaged children. At Seneca High, he developed remedial courses in English that prepared disadvantaged students for commercial and college track programs. He also initiated after school programs that provided cultural-enriching experiences (visiting museums, etc.) for disadvantaged students.

In his meetings with high school students and their parents, Terry was again confronted by bitter expressions of racial antagonism. While most white parents and students praised the faculty and programs at Seneca High, many also looked askance at that "liberal Jew, Fishbein, and his small clique of do-gooders with their special programs for the blacks." Similarly, while most black parents and students criticized the racist bent of the faculty and programs at Seneca High, many also praised that "small group of dedicated white teachers, led by Mr. Fishbein," who were "sensitive" to black needs and "tried" to meet them. Terry was particularly impressed by Louis Arron, an informed and articulate black student and an outstanding basketball player. Arron, the son of a poor mill worker was a natural leader and enjoyed considerable support from the black students. He was also a college-track student of above average ability who had benefited from the remedial courses and special programs offered by the Fishbein-led group of teachers. In his interview with Terry, he stressed his gratitude for those teachers who had helped him achieve college-track status, but he also expressed bitterness toward most other white teachers on the faculty for their reluctance in accepting him in the program and for their condescending attitude toward his performance in class. He felt they created a classroom environment in which he was viewed as a "black exception in a white world," "an aberration to be tolerated," and a "deviant from the slothful condition natural to blacks."

During the year that Hank Terry studied the Coalton District schools, his teenage son, Peter, had become a close friend of Board of Education President Michael Sloan's son, Winslow. On several occasions Winslow Sloan had dined at the Terry home, and Hank Terry had engaged in long discussions with him. In these exchanges Hank Terry was deeply disturbed by Winslow's hatred of blacks and the scornful and blatant hostility he expressed toward them. More frightening was the popularity he claimed among his white peers and the apparent leadership role he enjoyed because of the support his views received. So concerned was Hank Terry with Winslow's racist attitude and the prestige it had brought him, that he advised his son against accompanying Winslow to the game parlor which was located in the southern area of the Coalton School District (Fig. 5–1) and had been the scene of several altercations between black and white youths. But Peter Terry did not heed his father's advice, and late one afternoon in spring, both youths were among a group taken to the police station when a melee at the game parlor was broken up. However, a phone call by Winslow's father to the chief-of-police enabled both youths to be released before formal charges were made. Though Hank Terry later learned from Peter that Winslow Sloan had precipitated the incident, he was grateful for Michael Sloan's action and, in a personal note, thanked him for enabling his son to avoid the ignominy that an arrest and police record would have brought.

In his September 1st report to Superintendent Carns, Hank Terry detailed the highly explosive racial disharmony he had found festering among faculty and student body in the schools and among black and white parents in the community. He was particularly concerned with the "indifference of white administrators and faculty to the black community's escalating discontent and determination to be heard." He feared that an "environment" had been created in the high school that "invited racial confrontation, disorder, and possible violence." Terry concluded his report by urging immediate implementation of the following recommendations.

1. The Board of Education should draw up an integration-busing plan to achieve racial balance in the four elementary schools by September 1st of the following year.

2. The Coalton School District should actively engage in a program to recruit black teachers and administrators with the ultimate goal of employing eighteen to twenty-four percent of all personnel from this minority group.

3. All teachers and administrators in the Coalton School District should be required to attend workshops on teaching the disadvantaged and on working with racial minority groups.

4. A special committee of administrators, teachers, and parents should be appointed by the Board of Education to develop programs promoting racial harmony between schools and community.

Hank Terry's report was politely received by Superintendent Carns who promised to "study it carefully" over the next several months and to "take its recommendations under advisement," offering them as "possible directions" for his successor to consider. Superintendent Carns sought to ignore the warnings, fears, and sense of urgency Terry's report conveyed; he was certain he could bide his time until his retirement at the end of the school year without ever acting on the report. But events during the first week of school were to prove him wrong.

On the evening of the second day of school, a melee involving black and white students occurred at the game parlor. When the police arrived, the students dispersed quickly but only after several store windows were smashed. The following afternoon during the school lunch period, several fist fights broke out between black and white male students. Before the teachers monitoring the cafeteria could break them up, a major riot broke out. A large number of black and white male students threw chairs, overturned tables, smashed light fixtures, emptied garbage containers, and attacked each other with belts, pieces of broken furniture, knives, and lunch trays. Students not involved in the disturbance sought to escape into the corridors. But some of the rioting students followed them out and, roving the corridors in gangs of five or six, beat up anyone of an opposite color they came upon. Teachers stood by and watched helplessly as students inflicted an array of injuries upon each other that ranged from breaking noses and knocking out teeth to cuts, bruises, sprains, and contusions. As soon as the principal learned of the riot, he contacted the police, but they failed to respond immediately and arrived one-half hour later, well after most of the injuries and damage had occurred.

The day after the riot the Board of Education ordered an immediate investigation of the riot. It also instructed that state-mandated procedures be followed to insure a just and speedy trial of those involved in the disturbance. Under these procedures students charged with contributing to the riot were brought before Assistant Superintendent Terry who reviewed the evidence, abstracted "facts of finding" and presented, in writing, to Superintendent Carns key information involved in the case, an opinion of "guilty" or "innocent" and a recommendation of punishment. Superintendent Carns then "rubber-stamped" Terry's opinion and recommendation, and this became the final decision which could not be appealed. Each student brought up on charges was allowed a lawyer; many of the white students employed private lawyers while all of the black students were represented by ACLU lawyers. The attorney for the Board of Education acted as prosecutor, and a court stenographer recorded all that was said. In his role as judge Terry was advised by a state-assigned lawyer on making decisions relating to technicalities of law such as overriding objections, allowing admissable evidence, etc. Charges against students brought to trial were made by teachers who witnessed specific incidents in which the youths were involved. These teachers were subject to cross-examination by the defense lawyer for the student charged and were required to explain and defend their allegations. Students were either found innocent and cleared of all charges or were found guilty and suspended for six months to one year or dismissed from school permanently.

Twenty-eight students were brought up on charges: twenty were black, including Louis Arron; eight were white, including Winslow Sloan. Court proceedings lasted ten weeks, and at the end of each of these weeks, Terry submitted his findings, decision, and recommended punishment for two of the students charged. By the end of the ninth week, Terry had suggested rulings, and Superintendent Sloan had concurred, on all of the students except Louis Arron and Winslow Sloan. Of the nineteen black students charged, four were cleared, four were suspended for six months, eight were suspended for one year, and three were expelled permanently. Of the seven white students, two were cleared, two were suspended for six months, two were suspended for one year, and one was expelled permanently.

48

The remaining two cases proved the most difficult for Terry. The testimony of three white teachers charging Louis Arron with an active role in the rioting was seriously undermined by Arron's lawyer who established that most of Arron's action's were in self-defense. This position seemed to be corroborated further when two key defense witnesses, the basketball coach and Gerald Fishbein, testified that they had watched Arron "being attacked" and, in turn, "being forced to defend himself." However, the reliability of one of these witnesses was undermined when the prosecuting attorney successfully challenged parts of the basketball coach's testimony.

Winslow Sloan was charged by Gerald Fishbein with inciting a riot, willful destruction of school property, and assault and battery. Fishbein, who was on cafeteria duty the day of the riot, testified that prior to the outbreak of fighting he observed Winslow "taunting several black students" and "making obscene gestures" at them. He noted that in the course of the riot, Winslow "smashed furniture" and "clubbed two black students with part of a broken chair leg." He also testified that Winslow led a group of six white students who "ran around the school corridors beating up black students who were emptying their lockers in order to leave the buildings." Fishbein's allegations were sharply contested by four white teachers, not associated with the remedial programs to help blacks, who testified that Winslow sought to "avoid involvement in the disturbance" and reacted "purely in self-defense to black students who instigated the riot and attacked him." Though Fishbein resolutely defended his allegations against Winslow throughout a lengthy and intensive cross-examination by the defense lawyer, the reliability of his charges was somewhat diminished by the failure of the prosecuting attorney, in his brief cross-examination, to challenge statements by the four teachers that the youth acted solely in self-defense.

During the final days of testimony in the Arron and Sloan hearings, Board of Education President Michael Sloan requested a conference with Hank Terry. At this meeting, Sloan thanked Terry for responding with "alacrity to the demands of presiding over the difficult hearings" and praised him for the "decorum in which they were conducted" and for the "equitable decisions" that had resulted from his "unbiased, detached approach." He also praised Terry for the September 1st report which had "clearly defined the racial problems plaguing the Coalton School District" and had "accurately predicted the racial violence" that had occurred. Sloan also expressed considerable concern over conditions in the high school; an institution which he described as lying "between heaven and hell," geographically located on the imaginary line dividing the affluent white northern area of the school district, bordered by a seminary, from the poor, black southern area, bordered by a prison. He was anxious to "avoid further racial discord" and was certain a "return to normalcy" at the high school would ensue if Terry "quietly disposed" of the remaining two cases and found Louis Arron and his son innocent of all charges. He reminded Terry of the leadership position and popularity each of these youths enjoyed among their respective black and white peers, and he warned that a ruling against either of them would only "exacerbate the social disorder at the high school and produce further violence." He also noted that any disciplinary action taken against these students would jeopardize their future opportunities for admission and scholarships to higher institutions of learning. He concluded by informing Terry that he considered him to be the "logical choice" to succeed Superintendent Carns and that he was "certain" that Terry would "choose the most expeditious path" to defuse the crisis at Seneca High School. As Terry rose to leave, Michael Sloan extended his hand and said, "I have always sought to be of assistance when you and your son needed me; now I need your help!"

On the evening before Terry was to submit his findings and recommendations on Louis Arron and Winslow Sloan to Superintendent Carns, he reexamined the court stenographer's notes and carefully went over in his mind all that had happened during the court trials. In the Louis Arron case, he found the testimony by the white teachers filing charges against the youth to contain serious flaws and inconsistencies. In contrast, he was impressed by the ease with which Arron's defense lawyer was able to establish, through a number of witnesses, that his client had acted purely in self-defense. In the Winslow Sloan case, he was troubled that Fishbein's account of Winslow's actions was not corroborated by any other teacher. Yet, he was impressed by Fishbein's clear, coherent statement of charges against the youth and by his unshaken reaffirmation of these allegations throughout an intensive cross-examination. In contrast, he regretted the prosecuting attorney's rather brief cross-examination which left unchallenged the seemingly colorable testimony of those teachers supporting Wilson's self-defense claim.

From his extensive review of the case materials, Terry concluded that Louis Arron was innocent. In his suggested ruling to Superintendent Carns, he recommended that Arron be "cleared of all charges." Terry now had to make a ruling on Winslow Sloan: a decision which he recognized would have significant consequences for the future racial harmony of the school district, for the future academic plans of Winslow Sloan, and for his own future administrative career. Terry was confronted with a difficult decision. Should he find Winslow Sloan guilty and recommend disciplinary action or should he find Winslow Sloan innocent and recommend he be cleared of all charges? What should he do?

# Study Guide for Case #5

To the Instructor and Student:

This guide is designed to assist the student in analyzing this case in the following ways. It suggests:

1. a major *Area of Educational Concern* that is central to the case and upon which the student should focus his/her research efforts.

2. *Concepts* that are related to key dimensions of the case and that the student should seek to understand. These *Concepts* have broad implications for educational theory and practice and are listed as *Pivotal Terms.*

3. *Questions* that are concerned with problems raised by the case and that the student should explore further for possible issues;

4. *Reference Material* that is related to the case and that the student should use as a resource in researching the case;

## Case #5

### *"Between Heaven and Hell"*

1. *Area of Educational Concern:* Can school districts effectively achieve racial balance in their schools and promote equality of educational opportunity for all their students?

2. *Concepts-Pivotal Terms:*

| | |
|---|---|
| Brown vs. Bd. of Educ. (1953) | conflict theorists |
| allegations | suspended |
| disadvantaged social strata | racism |
| diversifying teaching strategies | racial subordination |
| non-racist society | equal opportunity employer |
| racial/social class stereotypes | integration-busing plan |
| expelled | ACLU |
| discriminatory school practices | NAACP |
| de facto segregation | school ethos |
| self-fulfilling prophecy | remedial courses |
| cultural-enriching experiences | minority |

3. *Questions:*

Should students involved in possible criminal behavior during school hours be tried by school officials or by judges in family/criminal courts?

Should school districts be forced to integrate schools where racial imbalances exist?

Is it possible to divorce politics from the process of selecting school administrators?

Is tenure an obstacle to efforts to require teachers to undergo retraining necessary to create a non-racist environment in the schools?

How can school personnel effectively promote harmonious school-community relationships?

Do schools preserve the status quo by separating the winners from the losers?

4. *Reference Material:*

Arans, Stephen and Lawrence III, Charles. (1982). The Manipulation of Consciousness, in Robert B. Everhart, ed., *The Public School Monopoly*. Cambridge, MA: Ballinger Publishing Company.

Fruchter, Norman. (1988). Needed: A new exchange relationship between students and schools. *Social Policy,* 19(1), 5–8.

Grant, Carl A. and Sleeter, Christine E. (1986). *After the School Bell Rings*. Philadelphia: The Falmer Press.

Holland, Spencer H. (1989). Staking a claim. *Social Policy,* 19(1), 13–16.

Meek, Anne. (1989). On Creating Ganas. *Educational Leadership,* 46 (5), 46–47.

Pressman, Harvey and Alan Gartner. (1986). The new racism. *Social Policy,* 17(1), 11–15.

Ravitch, Diane. (1979). Color-Blind or Color Conscious? *The New Republic,* 15–20.

Ravitch, Diane. (1989). Education and the Public Good. *Phi Kappa Phi Journal,* LXIX, 3, 35–38.

# A Parent's Help

John Silvera had always wanted to be a history teacher and applied himself diligently to his studies to prepare himself. He was class valedictorian at Tuck Latin High School and Phi Beta Kappa at State University, but he graduated during a time when the job market was depressed, and there were few teaching positions available. He, therefore, considered himself extremely fortunate when a position at Tuck unexpectedly opened, and he was selected for it from a large field of candidates.

John felt Tuck was an ideal place to teach. Its classical curriculum attracted a highly motivated, intellectually superior student body that usually gained admission to the finest universities in the region. The parents of Tuck students were chiefly from the professional sector, and they closely followed their children's progress in the schools. Teachers knew that when a child's academic performance slipped, they could rely upon concerned parents to cooperate with the school and provide whatever assistance was necessary in the home.

Tuck also had an experienced and well trained faculty. Among its most outstanding members were a husband and wife team, Robert and Janet Cell. Robert was chairman of the science department, and under his leadership it offered accelerated programs producing many state science fair winners and qualifying Tuck students for advanced placement in science courses at the universities. Robert had also been awarded federal grants for summer research projects, and his work at State University had result in several publications in prestigious national scientific journals. Janet Cell had a reputation as an excellent history teacher, and her roles as coordinator of the annual model legislature and teacher advisor to the History Club and Student Council had made her popular with students, parents, and teachers. The respect and esteem which the Cells enjoyed was reflected in their being the first joint recipients of the Outstanding Teacher's Award, the highest honor the state could confer on its teachers.

John Silvera looked forward to working with Janet Cell. During his years as a student at Tuck, he had been inspired by her understanding of history and her love of teaching. As president of the Student Council and the History Club, he had appreciated the wisdom of her counsel, the magnitude of her patience, and her genuine concern for the welfare of her students. Janet Cell had also been his supervising teacher during his student teaching field work, and he felt she had made it an extremely rich and rewarding experience.

John's first teaching assignment consisted of three classes in American History and two in Ancient History. The departmental requirements for each course had been carefully spelled out by the chairman, Phil Past. They included a basic text and a general syllabus that defined the material to be covered. John was expected to develop unit and daily lesson plans and to file copies of them with the chairman. He was also expected to give daily quizzes, six, one-hour unit exams, and a two-hour final. Copies of the unit and final exams were to be submitted to the chairman a week prior to administering them. A special departmental committee, chaired by Janet Cell, monitored all exams to insure they tested for the materials required in the course and met the standards of test construction expected by the history department.

Among the students in John's twelfth grade American History class was the Cell's only child, Pamela. She was the Cell's "pride and joy," and they expected her to continue on their path of scholarship and teaching. John found her to be a conscientious student of average ability who always prepared her homework assignments but rarely contributed to class discussions. He noted that in her responses on the daily quizzes she had considerable difficulty with thought questions that required abstracting, synthesizing, and interpreting material.

At the end of the third week of classes Pamela's daily quizzes averaged 78, and John held a conference with her after school concerning her performance. She told him that she liked his class and spent at least one hour each evening on her history homework. He complimented her on her preparation and effort, but he warned that she must participate in class discussion and move beyond a simple recitation of facts on her daily quizzes if she were to improve her grade. She became extremely upset as he spoke with her, and in a tear-choked voice told him that if she did not receive an A in American History she would not graduate on the state honor society because her cumulative grade average for her high school years would be less than B. She said that the admissions officer of the college of her choice—the one her parents wanted her to attend—had warned her that she could be rejected if she were not on the honor society. She reminded John that her mother had spoken with him earlier in the term and had offered to provide whatever extra assistance she might need. She said her parents were aware of her problem in history and that her mother was spending several hours each weekend helping her to abstract, synthesize, and interpret the material.

John was pleased to learn that Janet Cell was involved. He knew that she was the most qualified person to help Pamela with her problem; yet, he questioned whether even Janet's tutoring could bring Pamela's performance up to an A level. He sought to convey this uncertainty to Pamela by cautioning her that she might not be able to earn an A and that a B was a respectable grade, and she should be proud to receive it. He reminded her that the unit and final exams determined eighty percent of her grade and that she must receive at least a 92 on them if she were to earn an A in the course.

As time for the first unit exam in American History approached, John had the class practice writing essay questions. He required his students to always write a brief outline before developing the essay, a practice which he had learned from Janet Cell while he was a student teacher and which he felt insured clear, coherent, concise essays. On the day of the exam, John moved about the class checking the outlines students were developing on the inside of their exam booklet covers. He was particularly pleased with Pamela Cell's and felt they could lead to fine essays. She did not disappoint him and wrote excellent essays, receiving a 96, the highest grade in the class. When John returned the corrected tests, he used her exam as an example of how the essay questions should have been written. He recopied her outline on the board and had Pamela read her exam aloud. At the end of class John overheard one of the students remark, "I probably could have done as well if my mother were in the history department." John was disturbed by this comment but dismissed it as "sour grapes."

For the next three units, Pamela continued her erratic performance. She received 95 or better on her unit exams while she struggled to maintain an 80 average on her daily quizzes. John encouraged her to participate in class discussions but with little success. He had assigned her an A for each of the first two quarters, and he felt the class would benefit from her contributions.

Two days before the fifth unit exam, Pamela suddenly became ill in John's class and had to be taken home. In the confusion, she left her history notebook and text on her desk. As John gathered up these materials at the end of the period, he opened the notebook and examined its contents. He found a copy of each of the outlines Pamela had used so successfully in the first four unit exams. There was also an outline and rather detailed notes for the fifth exam which Pamela had yet to take. John was stunned. He had given the class several practice questions, but none of them could have led to Pamela's outline and notes which focused directly upon the exam question to be given.

John had always been concerned with the "security" of his exams and, consequently, typed and mimeographed them himself. The only copy that he released before the exam day was to the departmental committee that monitored the quality of tests—the committee headed by Janet Cell. Before leaving school that day, John received a message from the office: "Pamela Cell would be unable to attend class tomorrow. Her mother would pick up her history materials in the morning."

That evening John carefully weighed what had happened. He realized that he should not have examined Pamela's notebook without her permission. He also recognized that it was possible that Janet Cell, in tutoring her daughter, could have anticipated the general areas of history his questions would cover. Yet, the more he studied Pamela's outline, the more convinced he became that she must have had access to the specific exam questions. Further, he felt that Pamela's analysis of the question, as developed in her notes, reflected heavily her mother's level of critical thinking and in-depth understanding of material. John dreaded the conclusions he was drawing. Was it possible that Janet Cell, who had a copy of the exams a week before they were given, prepared her daughter for the questions by developing outlines and "fleshing them in" with notes on the necessary details? Was the explanation of Pamela's superb performance on the unit tests to be found in her having memorized outlines and notes prepared by her mother and having "simply fed them back" in essay form on the exam?

John was uncertain as to what action he should take. He realized the difficulty of his position. He was young, inexperienced, without tenure and new on the faculty. If he reported his findings and suggested his conclusions to Phil Past or asked Janet Cell for an explanation of the outline and notes he would, in effect, be challenging the professional integrity of one of the older, experienced, tenured, and most respected members of the faculty. This could lead to the ugly confrontation, accusations, controversy and divisiveness that would make it impossible for him to remain on the faculty at Tuck. If he chose to ignore what he had discovered, he felt he would be prostituting his own professional integrity and this could prove difficult to live with. What should he do? Should he report his findings and suggest his conclusions to Chairman Phil Past and/or ask Janet Cell for an explanation of the outline and notes or should he ignore his findings and say nothing?

# Study Guide for Case #6

To the Instructor and Student:

This guide is designed to assist the student in analyzing this case in the following ways. It suggests:

1. a major *Area of Educational Concern* that is central to the case and upon which the student should focus his/her research efforts.

2. *Concepts* that are related to key dimensions of the case and that the student should seek to understand. These *Concepts* have broad implications for educational theory and practice and are listed as *Pivotal Terms.*

3. *Questions* that are concerned with problems raised by the case and that the student should explore further for possible issues;

4. *Reference Material* that is related to the case and that the student should use as a resource in researching the case;

## Case #6

*"A Parent's Help"*

1. *Area of Educational Concern:* Should schools encourage parents to assist their children with their school work and, if so, is there a point at which such assistance becomes cheating?

2. *Concepts-Pivotal Terms:*

| | |
|---|---|
| tenure | professional ethics |
| essay type questions | teaching strategy |
| social stratification | faculty morale |
| cheating | parental involvement |
| right to privacy | In re Gault (1967) |
| unwarranted search | Fourth Amendment |
| student-teacher relations | "whistleblower" |
| alleged | advanced placement |
| model legislature | supervising teacher |
| unit/daily lesson plans | honor society |
| classical/prescribed curriculum | class participation |

3. *Questions:*

What role should students' rights play in the operations of the school?

Should lack of tenure affect a teacher's actions?

Should former students return to their schools for their student teaching experience and/or for their first teaching position?

Should professional ethics come before professional gain?

Does attending the same school where their parents are teachers or administrators create problems for students?

Should possible damage to faculty morale temper a "whistleblower's" action?

Should school searches based on suspicion of particular students be allowed?

What teacher practices would most effectively utilize parent involvement?

4. *Reference Material:*

Blatt, B. and Ozolens, A. (1982). On academic plague. *Journal of Learning Disabilities,* 15(9), 562–563.

Briggs, Dorothy C. (1975). *Your Child's Self-Esteem: The Key to Life.* New York: Doubleday.

Epstein, Joyce and Becker, Henry. (1982). Parent Involvement: A survey of teacher's practices. *Elementary School Journal,* 83(2), 85–102.

Johnson, Jeffrey L. and Donald W. Crowley, (1986). T.L.D. and the student's right to privacy. *Educational Theory,* 36(3), 211–223.

Lincoln, Eugene A. (1986). Searches and seizures: The U.S. Supreme Court's decision on the fourth amendment. *Urban Education,* 21(2), 254–62.

Morris, Samuel. (1980). Must children fail in school? *The Clearing House,* 54(1), 38–40.

Sendor, Benjamin. (1988). Courts agree: School searches should be based on suspicion of particular students. *American School Board Journal,* 175(1), 18–19.

# The Injury

Life had not been easy for Angela Rand, but she had persevered to overcome adversities that would have defeated others. The oldest child of a family of ten, she had delayed marrying until her mid-thirties, remaining at home to help support the family and often working at two jobs. The early years of her marriage were marred by financial difficulties as her husband, a World Ward II veteran, suffered from a service-related illness and was often unable to work. After the birth of her second child, her husband's health worsened, and Angela had to assume the burden of supporting the family. To prepare herself for a job that would insure security and a steady income, she enrolled in an evening program at college and pursued a teaching degree in elementary education. During the next six years, while she attended college on a part-time basis, she ran a day nursery in her home to support her family. Finally, at the age of forty-two she complete her degree work and accepted a position to teach a fifth grade class in Sonoma's North Street Elementary School.

Sonoma was a city in transition. Over a twenty-year period a large number of its affluent white families of professional workers had moved to neighboring communities. They had been replaced by poor white, Hispanic, and black families, often with single-parent households, who worked for marginal wages in service industries and in small plastics and jewelry factories that had sprung up in the decaying areas of the city. Prior to this change, Sonoma had boasted one of the finest school systems in the state. Sonoma's elected school committee, which was empowered to raise taxes to support education, had increased the tax rates frequently and spent money liberally to develop an effective school system designed primarily to prepare middle class students for college, management or technical careers. But with the population shift the school committee was confronted with a fiscal crisis triggered by a shrinking tax base and by a resistance from the remaining affluent taxpayers to fund costly programs to meet the needs of the newly-emergent minority and disadvantaged segments of the student population. School committee members, fearful of being voted out of office, failed to increase taxes to meet rising costs. Consequently, school buildings were allowed to deteriorate, needed programs languished, and school personnel salaries fell to the lowest in the state.

In addition to these mounting financial problems, the school committee was confronted by an increasingly vocal Hispanic minority which had grown to over twenty-five percent of the population and which demanded school personnel and programs more receptive to their needs. Responding to these demands, the school committee hired as superintendent, Dr. Alvarez Cordeira, a highly qualified and personable administrator of Hispanic parentage. It directed him to "recruit minority administrators and teachers" and to "develop programs to challenge minority and culturally disadvantaged students," but it failed to provide him with the necessary, additional funds to achieve these ends. Consequently, when the principal's position at North Street Elementary School became vacant, Cordeira lacked money to recruit outside the Sonoma school system and was forced to appoint Ramon Navaras, the only minority candidate available within the system.

Cordeira was uncertain of his choice though, on the surface, Navaras was an appealing candidate. He was a tall, handsome, suave, first-generation American of Spanish descent, thirty-four years old, married, and the father of four children. He was a ten-year, veteran teacher of the Sonoma school system, had earned a graduate degree in administration, spoke fluent Spanish and Portuguese, and was very popular in the Hispanic community where he was active in social, political, and church affairs. However, he was also reputed to be a "lady's man" and was rumored to have had several affairs with school personnel.

When Ramon Navaras became principal of North Street Elementary, Angela Rand had been teaching there for fifteen years and was one of the school's oldest and most effective teachers. She always demanded the highest quality of work from all her pupils, prepared her lessons carefully, and remained abreast of various teaching strategies. Thus, when her class filled with minority and disadvantaged pupils, she attended special workshops to learn how to challenge them. She maintained a warm, friendly relationship with her students, cultivating a classroom environment free of disciplinary problems based on mutual teacher-pupil respect. However, outside the classroom Rand sought to distance herself from others. She failed to develop meaningful relationships with her younger colleagues and, other than a few close friendships with older members of the faculty, she tended to be a loner. She was a private, reserved person, rarely revealing anything about her life and family and never commenting on school policy or the actions of her colleagues. Even the teacher aide, who worked closely with her in large classes of thirty-six students, never saw her relinquish her restrained, quite, understated quality.

During his first year as principal, Navaras delegated the responsibilities of routine school operations to the vice principal while he observed classes; instituted curriculum changes to meet the needs of minority and culturally disadvantaged students; initiated several programs focusing on cultural pluralism; met with parents; and revived the local chapter of the Parent-Teacher Association. He also engaged in a torrid, clandestine affair with Joanne Sak, a beautiful, young, popular teacher who was the president of the Sonoma teacher union. Many of his meetings with Sak took place in a neighborhood apartment during school hours while her teacher aide covered her classes. The affair ended in May but not before a student in Sak's afternoon recess class was injured while Sak was with Navaras and the class was being supervised only by the teacher aide. Navaras sought to cover up the incident and, on the insurance form filed by the injured student's parents, justified Sak's absence during the recess period by claiming she had become ill earlier in the day and he had taken her home. However, Superintendent Cordeira, who had heard rumors of the Navaras-Sak liaison and who was struggling to contain rising school insurance premiums, was angered by Navaras' explanation. In a sharply-worded memo he was highly critical of insurance claims that "seemed to be caused by administrative negligence," and he warned of the "possibility of malfeasance."

Despite this incident, Cordeira was favorably impressed with Navaras' first year performance. He had received numerous letters from civic and church leaders in the poor white, black, and Hispanic communities praising Navaras' administrative efforts. They credited him with "encouraging understanding through cultural awareness programs" and with promoting the "educational welfare" of minority students and of disadvantaged white students through curriculum reform. Cordeira was also pleased with the favorable publicity Navaras received in the local newspaper when he was selected Regional Catholic of the Year for his church work and when he was singled out for special recognition by the Parent-Teacher Association for his work in reestablishing their local chapter.

During his second year as principal, Navaras continued to promote programs to help minority students, specifically white disadvantaged children who had participated in Project Head Start. His efforts met increasing resistance from the younger faculty who were ill-prepared to teach minority and disadvantaged students, who viewed special programs for such students as being developed at the expense of quality educational programs needed by the majority of white affluent students, and who resented Navaras' grandstanding with school programs to enhance his reputation with the community leaders. Only Angela Rand cooperated fully with Navaras, devoting considerable time and effort to develop creative and exciting lessons for the minority and disadvantaged. So well-designed were these lessons that Navaras, after praising Rand for her "ingenuity" at a faculty meeting, distributed copies of her lessons as models for other teachers to follow. Rand's support of Navaras' efforts further isolated her from the younger faculty who had never felt comfortable with her reticent, aloof manner and who were now convinced she was attempting to ingratiate herself with the principal at their expense.

This period of harmony and cooperation between Navaras and Rand was shortlived. Early in the school year Navaras began a surreptitious affair with Rand's teacher aide, a married mother of two children. The liaison was carried on in a neighborhood apartment during afternoon school hours; consequently, Rand taught her classes without the required assistance. Rand never commented on her aide's frequent absences from class though it left her alone to supervise a large number of students in the difficult afternoon recess period. On a Friday afternoon in the first week of October while Rand was lining up students after the recess bell had rung, a student standing several feet behind Rand kicked a soccer ball that struck her with considerable force in the back of the neck. Rand collapsed, remaining on the ground in a semiconscious state until a teacher, Alice Dawson, summoned by one of the students, helped her stagger to the principal's office. Dawson, a close friend and long-time teaching associate, made Rand comfortable while the principal's secretary, unable to reach the vice principal, ran around the building looking for Navaras. When this search proved futile, Rand filled out an accident form required by the school insurance policy and with Dawson's help returned to her classroom. Rand managed to complete the school day, but that evening she became dizzy and nauseous and was taken to the emergency room of the local hospital where she was placed on medication and directed to be ex-rayed by an orthopedic surgeon.

Long after Rand left the building on Friday afternoon, Navaras returned to find the accident report on his desk and to learn of the incident from his perplexed secretary who complained that she "tried in vain to find him during the emergency." Navaras, realizing the vulnerability of his position, claimed he was in the building at the time conferring with teacher-union president Joanne Sak. He ridiculed his secretary for her "emotionalism" and reprimanded her for failing to locate him. He also destroyed the accident report and, in all future inquiries regarding it, steadfastly maintained that "to his knowledge, an accident report had never been filed."

When Rand returned to school on Monday she was confronted by a hostile Navaras who belittled the seriousness of her injury and refused to release her during school time the be ex-rayed by an orthopedic surgeon. She also learned that her teacher aide was taking a personal leave of absence and would not be available for the remainder of the school year. In a brief note her aide apologized for her unexcused absences from afternoon classes and explained that "recurring family problems had unexpectedly arisen that required her presence." For the next three months, Navaras continued to obstruct Rand's efforts to receive medical attention during school time while stonewalling all negotiations relating to the accident. When Rand required physical therapy treatments during school hours, Navaras refused to assign another teacher to her classes. She was able to attend the therapy sessions only after the vice principal intervened and taught her classes. Similarly, when the school's insurance company refused to "acknowledge liability" for the accident, claiming that an "accident report had never been filed," Navaras supported the company, affirming that he had "never forwarded the insurance company such a form because one had never crossed his desk," Without this report, a claim could not be acted on; therefore Rand, despite her protestations, was required to file another report several weeks after the accident occurred. The insurance company in turn questioned the "seriousness and legitimacy of an accident and injury which had been reported so belatedly."

Shortly before Christmas vacation Rand, who continued to have dizzy spells and experienced numbness on the left side of her body, suffered an allergic reaction to medication prescribed because of the injury and was hospitalized. While at the hospital she underwent a series of tests which raised questions as to whether she would ever recover fully from the injury. Confronted with mounting medical bills, suffering from a partial paralysis of her left side, and faced with the prospect of an injury causing progressive damage to her health, a frightened and emotionally-drained Rand retained a lawyer to protect her interests. Within a week her lawyer had filed a suit against the school system and the school insurance company seeking a settlement that would "compensate his client for the pain, damage to health, and loss of potential income" resulting from the injury. The suit detailed the events surrounding the accident and charged Ramon Navaras with "administrative negligence" which contributed directly to its occurrence.

Superintendent Cordeira responded to the lawsuit by launching an intensive investigation into the causes of Rand's accident and the extent of her injury. As superintendent, he was required by state law to judge school personnel who were formally charged with misconduct or negligence and to determine, when necessary, disciplinary action to be taken. His decision would ultimately determine the outcome of Rand's lawsuit. If he found Navaras guilty of negligence and disciplined him, Rand would receive a large settlement and the insurance company would not take the case to trial. But if he found Navaras innocent, Rand would be offered a nominal settlement or face the prospect of a long and expensive litigious battle with the insurance company.

To facilitate his investigation, Cordeira directed the assistant superintendent and the school lawyer to examine all facets of the Rand accident, to interview all person familiar with any aspect of the incident, and to report their findings by October 1st. While this investigation was in process, the school insurance company, through its doctors, sought to determine the nature of Rand's injury and to minimize the seriousness of it. They required her to undergo a series of treatments ranging from psychiatric therapy to accupuncture in an effort to establish that her physical and emotional problems were not related to the accident.

During this second half of the school year, Rand found herself alone and miserable. Not only was she hounded by insurance company doctors and harassed by her principal, but she remained suspect with her fellow teachers. Most of the younger faculty, resenting her aloofness and what they viewed as her "eagerness' to comply with Navaras' "questionable approach" to curriculum reform, were secretly enjoying her difficulties. They felt Rand and Navaras "deserved each other," and the had little sympathy for whatever hardship and misery either party suffered. This antipathy towards Rand was reinforced by teacher-union president Joanne Sak who spread the rumor that Rand was faking her injury to get early retirement and a huge settlement. She warned that this would raise school insurance rates which would further deplete school revenue needed for future faculty pay raises. Only Rand's close friend, Alice Dawson, defended the injured teacher's actions, and though Dawson was popular and respected, she was able to dissuade few among the faculty. But events in May were to change all this.

Shortly before the end of the school year, the school committee, responding to taxpayer pressure, sought to contain requests for budget increases to avoid raising the tax rate. It therefore refused the Sonoma teacher union demands for a sizable pay increase. The union's executive committee called for a strike vote, but before it could be taken, president Joanne Sak and a group of teachers who opposed the action, bolted from the organization. Alice Dawson was chosen to replace Sak, and under her leadership, union members engaged in a successful work stoppage that forced the school committee to satisfy their salary demands. During the eight days of the strike, Rand fully supported the job action by picketing, running a phone bank, and allowing her home to be used as a regular meeting place for her striking colleagues. By the end of the strike, Rand had gained acceptance among younger faculty who sympathized with her health problems and became supportive of her legal action against the school system.

Throughout the summer months and the early weeks of September, the assistant superintendent and school lawyer conducted an exhaustive investigation of the Rand accident, interviewing most of the personnel at the North Street Elementary School. In their report to Superintendent Cordeira they acknowledged that it was impossible to provide an accurate account of what happened on the day of the accident and thereafter because questions surrounding four critical incidents within the chain of events were marked by conflicting testimony: why was the teacher aide absent from class; where was Navaras at the time of the accident; when did Rand file an accident report; and did Navaras harass Rand after the accident? The report found that while the younger faculty led by Alice Dawson supported Rand's version of what occurred, other faculty led by Joanne Sak supported Navaras' version. The report concluded with the following observations. First, many of the faculty viewed Navaras with contempt and felt that "somehow" his rumored affairs "contributed directly" to Rand's accident. However, the origins of much of the hostility of these teachers could be traced not to their distaste for Navaras' liaisons but to their dislike of Navaras' curriculum reforms which they resisted because they were unsympathetic to the needs of minority and disadvantaged students. Second, no *prima facie* evidence was found that definitely established that Navaras engaged in secret love affairs with school personnel during school time. However, considerable circumstantial evidence pointed to the possibility that such liaisons may have occurred. Third, Navaras' treatment of Rand was "permissible" within the purview of his authority as principal. However, in view of the "reasonableness" of Rand's requests (e.g., release from class for therapy sessions, etc.) many of his actions appeared to be "punitive and unnecessary."

Cordeira was to render a decision by the first week of November. Shortly before the day it was due, he was summoned to a meeting by the school committee chairman who expressed considerable concern that Cordeira would rule Navaras guilty of administrative negligence and discipline him. The chairman feared that such a decision would require the school insurance company to make a costly settlement with Rand and, in turn, to raise insurance premiums dramatically. This would force the school committee to retrench programs for minority and disadvantaged students in order to free funds for the premium increase. The chairman also reminded the superintendent of the considerable popularity and support Navaras enjoyed from influential segments of the community, and he warned that it would be difficult to justify a renewal of Cordeira's contract if this group were to be alienated by discipline action taken against the principal.

On the evening before his decision was due, Cordeira carefully reviewed all that had been written and said. He realized that his decision would have far-reaching beneficial or adverse consequences for a large variety of people with different interests. It would determine in large part the outcome of Rand's lawsuit, the status of Navaras' principleship, Cordeira's term of office, the financial support of special educational programs for disadvantaged and minority students, and the harmony of school-community relations.

Cordeira had a difficult decision to make. Should he find Navaras guilty of administrative negligence and discipline him, assuring Rand of a large settlement for her injury? Or should he rule Navaras innocent of administrative negligence, leaving Rand with a small settlement or a long and expensive litigious battle with the insurance company? What should he do?

# *Study Guide for Case #7*

To the Instructor and Student:

This guide is designed to assist the student in analyzing this case in the following ways. It suggests:

1. a major *Area of Educational Concern* that is central to the case and upon which the student should focus his/her research efforts.

2. *Concepts* that are related to key dimensions of the case and that the student should seek to understand. These *Concepts* have broad implications for educational theory and practice and are listed as *Pivotal Terms*.

3. *Questions* that are concerned with problems raised by the case and that the student should explore further for possible issues.

4. *Reference Material* that is related to the case and that the student should use as a resource in researching the case.

### Case #7

*"The Injury"*

1. *Area of Educational Concern:* What responsibility does a school have for the health and welfare of its personnel and, specifically, for personnel injured on the job?

2. *Concepts-Pivotal Terms:*

| | |
|---|---|
| cultural diversity | disadvantaged child |
| malfeasance | administrative negligence |
| minority | prima facie evidence |
| teacher strike | school-community relations |
| teacher aide | moral misconduct |
| teacher-pupil ratio | Project Head Start |
| Parent Teacher Association | labeling |
| equal opportunity employer | harassment |
| colleague relationships | liability |
| faculty morale | socialization |

72

3. *Questions:*

Should teachers be allowed to strike?

How responsive to community needs should a school be in developing programs?

What recourse should teachers have to administrative harassment or misconduct?

Should school committees be empowered to raise taxes to support education?

What would be the most effective way to evaluate administrators?

Should school principals have tenure?

Should school personnel be allowed to sue school systems?

4. *Reference Material:*

Becker, H. S. (1952). Social class variations in the teacher-pupil relationship. *Journal of Educational Sociology,* 25(2), 451–465.

Blumberg, Arthur. (1985). *The School Superintendent: Living with Conflict.* New York: Teachers College Press.

Callahan, R. E. (1962). *Education and the Cult of Efficiency.* Chicago: University of Chicago Press.

Edmonds, Ronald R. (1979). Some schools work and more can. *Social Policy,* 9(5), 28–32.

Fructure, Norm. (1985). Should principals have tenure? *Social Policy,* 16(2), 51–52.

Hodges, Michael. (1987). Children in the wilderness. *Social Policy,* 17(4), 43–47.

Mann, Danial. (1985). Effective schools for the poor. *Education Digest,* 5(7), 25–26.

Van Cleve Morris et al. (1984). Principals in Action. Columbus, OH: Charles E. Merrill.

# Stephen Lowe

Hamilton High was one of four high schools in the rapidly developing suburb of Seating Hills. It was built to accommodate the population growth that had resulted from an automobile assembly plant locating in the area. Its students were drawn from a broad cross section of professional, clerical, and working class families, and approximately one quarter of its graduates went to college while the remainder completed programs in business, industrial arts, and shop.

Hamilton High employed four guidance teachers to counsel its sixteen hundred students. Among them was Stan Lyzinski who had been on the faculty for eight years and had guided freshman classes twice through the four-year cycle to graduation. He was extremely conscientious in his work, sought to divide his time equally among all his advisees, and often remained after school to help them. He interviewed them, subjected them to a battery of interest and personality tests, and developed a folder on each of them which included anecdotal notes from their teachers plus his own comments on their visits to his office concerning academic problems, etc.

Stan enjoyed working with his advisees, was very popular, and had acquired a reputation of always being available when needed. He prided himself in knowing each of them rather well and in helping them through the trials and tribulations of their high school years and through the agony of their decision making in planning careers. All of this changed in Stan's ninth year as a guidance teacher when Stephen Lowe was among the advisees in the freshman class assigned to him.

Stephen Lowe was a bastard. His mother was unwed and only fifteen years old when he was born. She chose to keep her son and, with the help of welfare payments (Aid to Families with Dependent Children), she raised him alone and never married. When Stephen

75

first entered school, she became a waitress at her uncle's cafe and lived with her son in a small room above it. Stephen also helped in the cafe, and by the time he entered high school, he was busing tables and washing dishes every night of the week.

During his first eight years of schooling, Stephen displayed little interest in his work, did only the minimum of what was required, and was truant frequently. When he entered Hamilton High, he was placed in a general program with shop courses, and along with the other new students, he was given a battery of tests (intelligence, achievement, personality, aptitude) by the guidance department. A month after school began, Stan received the test scores for freshman class, and he was surprised by Stephen's performance. The test results indicated that Stephen was a gifted child of extremely high intelligence with high aptitude in the maths and sciences.

Stan carefully studied Stephen's records before meeting with him. He was disturbed by the failure of the schools to recognize and challenge an individual of such exceptional ability, and he was disappointed by the boy's environment which appeared to encourage his apathy toward school. Stan felt that Stephen must be made cognizant of his ability and be given every opportunity to exploit it fully. At his meeting with Stephen, Stan found him to be serious, polite and quite withdrawn. Stephen acknowledged that he had few friends and that his job at the restaurant allowed little time for homework. He admitted that he was glad to be in a general program because it demanded little of him and that he was biding his time until his sophomore year when he would drop out of school on his sixteenth birthday.

Throughout the following month, Stan met with Stephen regularly after school. He explained the meaning of the test scores, suggested possible academic programs Stephen might pursue, and provided him with an abundance of materials on professional areas that would be open to someone of his ability. By the end of the first quarter, Stan had developed an excellent counselor-pupil relationship with him, and Stephen dropped his general program and enrolled in college preparatory courses in English, math, science and history. For the remainder of the school year, Stephen studied in Stan's office before and after school. He frequently confided in the counselor and found Stan to be a father figure who believed in him and who was kind, patient, and understanding.

While Stan enjoyed the opportunity to do individual counseling with Stephen, it proved time consuming, and he found it increasingly difficult to meet with his other advisees. He frequently cancelled and delayed appointments or was not available in his office for advisees with scheduling problems or who were seeking information on careers, college admission, scholarships, etc. A growing number of students complained that they were "unaware of opportunities" or "missed deadlines" for applications because they "gave up trying to see Lyzinski." Many of these students turned to the other counselors for help, and this caused considerable discontentment among the staff. They disagreed with Stan's approach to counseling, and they complained to the principal, Mae Watterson, that they objected to "doing his work" when they already had an "overload of advisees requiring assistance". When Mae Watterson hesitated to act on their complaint, they took matters into their own hands. At a faculty meeting near the end of the school year, they openly raised the issue of Stan's failure to meet with his advisees. A heated exchange followed in which Stan attacked their "insensitivity" while defending his "response" to the special needs of an individual student. In turn, they criticized Stan for "neglecting the bulk" of his students while "playing Freud, God, and father" to one student. Further, they warned Stan that as of the new school year in September they would no longer "carry his load" and would meet only with their own advisees.

In addition to this growing rift with his colleagues, Stan was also concerned that his counseling of Stephen was complicating the boy's relationship with his mother. Stephen confessed to Stan that he had argued bitterly with her when he switched programs at school without her consent and that she constantly complained that he was "never home enough" to do his chores adequately. Stephen regretted that he was having difficulty communicating with her, but he did not agree with her accusation that his schoolwork was to blame and that Stan was "driving a wedge between them, destroying the close relationship they had always enjoyed." Rather, Stephen felt that his mother was "jealous of Stan" and that she "resented" his newly-discovered, gifted status and his talk of college and a professional career. Stan sought to repair this growing rift between mother and son and between parent and counselor. He wrote several letters and reports to Ms. Lowe praising her son's upbringing and abilities, describing the academic programs Stephen was enrolled in, and suggesting career opportunities that could be pursued. He also invited her to school to discuss her son's academic future, but she refused to come.

At the end of his freshman year, Stephen received a straight A report card, and Stan was elated. But his joy was shortlived. Principal

Mae Watterson, had received a letter from Stephen's mother in which she complained of Stan's interference in the upbringing of her child. She noted that her son spent excessive amounts of time at school, that he had lost all interest in his duties and responsibilities to her at home, and that she found it increasingly difficult to talk to him. She stated that she loved her son, that she had made considerable sacrifices in raising him without a father, that she knew what was best for him, and that she was not about to have an "outsider" step in and make the critical decisions affecting her son's future. She requested that Stan no longer work with her son and that a different counselor be assigned to Stephen. She concluded with a warning that Stephen was her legal responsibility ad that she would take whatever steps necessary to preserve her rights as a parent. She asked for a decision in writing from the principal within a week.

Mae Watterson was in total agreement with all that Stan was trying to do for Stephen, but she was also aware of Ms. Lowe's rights as a parent. Furthermore, while she was sympathetic to Stephen's continuing need for Stan's support and understanding, she was becomingly increasingly concerned with the infighting disrupting the counseling staff and with a growing number of complaints from Stan's advisees and their parents that the counselor was not available when needed.

A week after school had ended, Mae held a conference with Stan. She informed him of the contents of Ms. Lowe's letter, and she suggested that perhaps he should no longer serve as Stephen's counselor. She praised Stan for his efforts with Stephen, but she noted that the boy demanded too much of his time and that this was unfair to his other advisees who were also in need of his counsel. She reminded Stan that Stephen was only fifteen and, as a minor, was the legal responsibility of his parent who fed, clothed, and sheltered him. Stan acknowledged Ms. Lowe's rights as a parent, but he questioned whether the school did not have a greater right or responsibility to provide the most challenging education possible for such an exceptionally bright child. He also expressed regret that he had "differences" with his colleagues and that he had neglected his other advisees, but he questioned the justice of a school policy that in seeking to satisfy the demands of the many would patently ignore the needs of the one. Stan ended the discussion with an eloquent plea that he be allowed to continue as Stephen's counselor.

Mae Watterson was confronted with an extremely difficult decision. Should she concur with Ms. Lowe's requests and appoint a new counselor, or should she deny the request and retain Stan as Stephen's counselor? She must make a decision by the end of the week. What should she do?

# Study Guide for Case #8

To the Instructor and Student::

This guide is designed to assist the student in analyzing this case in the following ways. It suggests:

1. a major *Area of Education Concern* that is central to the case and upon which the student should focus his/her research efforts.

2. *Concepts* that are related to key dimensions of the case and that the student should seek to understand. These *Concepts* have broad implications for educational theory and practice and are listed as *Pivotal Terms.*

3. *Questions* that are concerned with problems raised by the case and that the student should explore further for possible issues;

4. *Reference Material* that is related to the case and that the student should use as a resource in researching the case;

## Case #8
### *"Stephen Lowe"*

1. *Area of Educational Concern:* Does an educator have a responsibility to meet the special needs of the one student when such actions may be at the expense of meeting the general needs of the many students?

2. *Concepts-Pivotal Terms:*

| | |
|---|---|
| *parens patriae* | gifted child |
| socialization | tracking |
| labeling | child advocacy |
| intelligence testing | disadvantaged |
| parental rights | dropout |
| counseling | personality tests |
| anecdotal notes | AFDC |
| truant | aptitude tests |
| single-parent family | rapport |
| general program | career opportunities |
| privacy/independence of family | age of consent |

3. *Questions:*

What are the responsibilities of parents/family versus those of professional educators/state in determining the educational needs/welfare of children?

What should be the role and goals of a counselor working with advisees who have home problems affecting school performance?

Should there be special counseling and guidance services for gifted children?

Who should decide when the rights of a child conflict with the rights of a parent?

How effective are schools in coping with students who plan to leave before completing their diploma requirements?

How effective have the schools been in challenging the bright underachievers?

4. *Reference Material:*

DeJames, Patricia L. (1982). Effective parent/teacher/child relationships. *Education,* 102(1), 34–36.

Fine, Michelle. (1985). Dropping out of high school: An inside look. *Social Policy,* 16(2), 43–50.

Glaser, Robert. (1977). Adapting to individual differences. *Social Policy,* 8(2), 27–33.

Goldberg, Miriam L. and Jane B. Raph. (1966). *Bright Underachievers,* New York: Teachers College Press.

Greer, Colin. (1969). Public Schools: The myth of the melting pot. *Saturday Review,* 52.), 84–86.

Lombana, Judy H. (1985). Guidance accountability: A new look at an old problem. *School Counselor,* 32(5), 340–346.

Phillips, Mark. (1976). Confluent education, the hidden curriculum, and the gifted child. *Phi Delta Kappa,* 58(3), 238–240.

Ritty, J. M. and Frost, M. B. (1985). Single parent families: How can schools help? *PTA Today,* 10(6), 14–15.

Sametz, Lynn and C. S. McLoughlin. (Eds.) (1985). *Educators, Children, and the Law.* Springfield, Illinois: Charles C. Thomas.

# For the Love of Joseph

Benjamin Warren Smith would be appointed the first black principal in Coleville. It was a foregone conclusion that when the principal of Coleville West High School resigned in two years, Ben would succeed him. Ben was chairperson of the History Department at Coleville West High, and he had proven himself an effective administrator and a concerned, informed teacher. He was respected by the faculty and administration, proved popular with the students, and enjoyed strong parental support. He was also viewed as the perfect role model for black students who made up fifteen percent of the student population, and he was constantly referred to by apologists for Coleville's questionable hiring policies as proof that "qualified blacks" can succeed in the system.

Ben had married Flora Robertson who was an elementary school teacher and the only other black ever employed by the Coleville school system. During the first ten years of their marriage, Ben pursued graduate studies in administration on a part-time basis while raising a family of three children. These were difficult years. Flora suffered a postpartum psychosis after the birth of her first child, Joseph, and again after her third child, Dalena. Each time she was hospitalized and required considerable psychiatric treatment. Ben found it difficult to meet the expenses incurred by these illnesses on his teacher's pay, and he had fallen deeply in debt. He looked forward to assuming a principalship with its more lucrative salary that would enable him to improve his financial situation.

The Coleville school system was headed by Phil Grafton. He had been appointed superintendent and given a three-year renewable contract because his close friend John Molitor, a powerful political figure, became chairperson of the school committee. Molitor had also been instrumental in the appointment of Phil's younger brother, Bill, to Director of Testing and Special Education Programs.

The Grafton brothers were opposites in every way. Phil was bright, articulate, personable, and a shrewd political animal. He recognized that renewal of his contract as superintendent relied upon Molitor retaining control over the school committee; therefore, he was supportive of Molitor and sought to curry favor with the school committee members. Phil exuded a charm that ingratiated him with all. He was quick to praise his colleagues and to acknowledge the contributions of parents and community leaders to the school programs. He also enjoyed the unswerving loyalty and support of a small but vocal group of faculty and administrators he had appointed, promoted or granted sundry favors.

Bill Grafton, in contrast to his brother, was slow, withdrawn, pedantic, and inflexible. He remained aloof from most people and isolated from his staff. He had few supporters, and his qualifications and competency had been challenged on several occasions by faculty and parents. He had survived because the superintendent's office never acted upon complaints leveled against him or his administration of the testing and special education programs.

In the fall of Benjamin Warren Smith's eleventh year of teaching, his oldest child, Joseph, entered kindergarten. Joseph was a shy, poorly coordinated child who seemed to be a slow learner but who responded favorably to individual attention. Flora prepared him for school by devoting countless hours to exercizes directed at reading readiness, math skills, and socialization skills. Joseph profited from his mother's tutoring and performed adequately in kindergarten. His teacher found him to be "conscientious and sincere," but she noted that he was poorly coordinated and "displayed hyperactive behavior when subjected to pressure." In September of the following year, Joseph entered Kay Molitor's first grade class.

Kay Molitor was the older sister of John Molitor and, like her brother, had been active in politics all her life. She had headed the campaign committees of a major party several times, and she had served as a delegate to both local and national conventions. Her teaching career of forty-two years had been highlighted by her introduction of a "happy house" in her classes. The "happy house" was a section of the classroom that had been partitioned off and that contained a large collection of the most recent, interesting, challenging, exciting, educational toys and games available on the market. Kay had purchased them with her own money, and she replaced and maintained them at considerable personal expense.

In theory, all students were allowed to visit the "happy house" and enjoy its games and toys each time they performed well on tests, showed growth and improvement in study and socialization skills, or made an outstanding contribution to class activities. In practice, the most frequent visitors to the "happy house" were a select few among the brighter students whom Kay enjoyed teaching and favored over the bulk of the students of average or lesser ability. The "happy house" remained popular among parents who did not understand its true nature. And, they tended to view it favorably, especially after it received considerable acclaim in the local newspaper. It was reported that the superintendent's office singled out Kay for her "generosity and creativity" in developing "an innovative educational tool" that "motivated students" and "rewarded effort appropriately."

Young Joseph Smith quickly fell into disfavor with Kay Molitor and never enjoyed a visit to the "happy house." He reverted to hyperactive behavior when Kay Molitor, displaying impatience with his slow responses and poor physical coordination, ridiculed him before the other children in class. Within two weeks after school began, Kay wanted Joseph removed from her class and had Bill Grafton test him. Bill found Joseph to be a "slow child" who was "educable," "hyperactive," and "socially backward." He recommended that Joseph be placed in a special education class and that he not be mainstreamed in regular classes unless he took medication (tranquilizers).

The Smiths refused to accept the test results and sought a second opinion from the psychiatrist who had treated Flora. In his examination, which included a battery of tests administered by his colleagues who were specialists in child learning, he found that Joseph had strabismus, a misalignment of the eyes, and that, consequently, he was "handicapped by a perceptual problem" and "labored under a learning disability" that affected his performance in school. The psychiatrist rejected Bill Grafton's findings and recommendations as "quackery," and he was highly critical of Coleville's testing and special education program. He noted that Joseph was not the first child to suffer from incorrect testing and faulty referrals. Rather, several of his patients had been victims of Bill Grafton's failure to test properly, and to establish and monitor quality programs to meet the special needs of exceptional children as required by P.L. 94–142. He also expressed dismay at the failure of the superintendent's office to act on the several complaints that he, and the parents of the children involved, had filed against Bill Grafton.

The psychiatrist recommended that Joseph be withdrawn from school for one year. During this time corrective surgery would be performed on Joseph's eyes, and he would undergo post-operative therapy which would focus upon a Montessori approach to learning "emphasizing tactile experiencing." The Smiths complied with these recommendations, and after Joseph underwent successful surgery, Flora provided the necessary post-operative therapy. She was assisted by a teacher from a private nursery that used the Montessori method. Joseph responded favorably to the therapy, and by the end of the year he was reading above the first grade level and displayed similar growth and development in skills and ability in the areas of writing and math. Some problems with his coordination remained, and he retained his shy and socially awkward demeanor.

The following September, Joseph's return to school was marred by a bitter dispute: his parents and his psychiatrist wanted him placed in a regular first grade class, but Bill Grafton and Kay Molitor sought to have him assigned to a nongraded special education class. To end this conflict, Superintendent Phil Grafton intervened and placed Joseph for an eight-week trial period in Kay Molitor's regular first grade class. He directed her to file a report at the end of this period on Joseph's progress and to make a recommendation as to whether he should remain in her class or be assigned to a special education class. Throughout this trial period Joseph said little to his parents about his classroom experiences and, because of their dispute with Kay Molitor, they were unable to learn anything concerning his class performance from her. Flora continued to work with Joseph after school and on weekends, and she remained very encouraged by his growth and improvement in mastering the 3Rs.

At the end of the trial period, Kay Molitor reported to Superintendent Phil Grafton that Joseph was "an extremely slow learner" who "totally lacked skills in the 3Rs" and who "frequently displayed hyperactive behavior." She repeated the recommendation that Bill Grafton had made the previous year that Joseph be placed in a special education class and that he be required to take medication (tranquilizers) before being mainstreamed. However, before Superintendent Phil Grafton could act on her recommendations, Kay Molitor was involved in a serious automobile accident in which her brother John was killed, and she was hospitalized for five weeks. In the shock and confusion that followed, Phil Grafton neglected to have Joseph Smith transferred to the special education class.

Melissa Mitchell was the long-term substitute who replaced Kay Molitor. She had earned an undergraduate degree in elementary education and a graduate degree in special education. She was an outstanding teacher who had acquired considerable expertise in working with exceptional children while teaching in several quality special education programs in a large city school system on the west coast. She had come to Coleville with her daughter to start a new life after her unhappy marriage had ended when her husband deserted them. Superintendent Phil Grafton was anxious to hire her because the Coleville school system lacked teachers with her credentials and was not meeting fully the state-mandated regulations to insure compliance with P.L. 94–142 requirements. Melissa, as a self-supporting, single-parent female, was anxious to attain the job security and income that a full-time, tenure-track, teaching position would bring. She had been assured by Phil Grafton that she would be hired when the next job opening occurred, and she had agreed to do substitute teaching until that time.

Melissa knew nothing about the controversy surrounding Joseph Smith's presence in the class. She had heard about the "happy house" and how it served as an incentive for students to excel. She was, therefore, very surprised when she entered class on the first day to find Joseph and two other boys not playing games but doing their lessons while seated at tables in the "happy house." She was stunned when two of the brighter children in class informed her that Miss Molitor allowed them to visit the "happy house" regularly and that they would "be careful" not to let the "dummies in there" play the games with them. Melissa allowed the children to visit the "happy house," but throughout the morning lessons she moved among the children in class and discretely made inquiries about the "happy house." She learned that the brightest children visited and played games on a regular schedule, that the average students were occasionally rewarded with a visit and played games, but that the slowest students, who in anyway disrupted the class, were confined to the "happy house" most of the day and never allowed to touch the toys and games. That afternoon, Melissa arranged her lessons so that she was free to work with the three children who had been isolated in the "happy house." She found that Joseph was above average in ability, responded favorably to warmth and attention, but became frightened, uncertain, and reverted to hyperactive behavior when confronted with hostility or felt threatened. She found the other two children were below average in ability and tended to become distracted, restless, and disruptive when they were confused or did not understand the lesson being taught.

That evening Melissa removed all the games and toys from the "happy house" and stored them in a closet. The next morning she announced to the class that the "happy house" was closed until Miss Molitor returned and that all students would be expected to do their lessons at their assigned seats. In the days that followed, Melissa arranged her lessons so that she could do individual work with the three children who had been isolated in the "happy house." She was particularly pleased with the progress Joseph made and quite surprised at the level of development of his skills in the 3Rs. At the end of four weeks she tested Joseph on these skills and found that he scored above the second grade level in all of them. Melissa had developed an excellent rapport with Joseph, and by carefully questioning him, she learned of the endless hours of lessons, built around patience, love, and understanding, that his mother had given him over the past three years. On the last day of her substitute assignment, Melissa wrote a letter to Flora praising her tutoring efforts with Joseph, pointing out the high scores he had received on the tests, noting that he was a "pleasure to have in class," and urging her to continue to work with him.

The following week Kay Molitor returned to work, and Joseph was promptly transferred to a nongraded special education class. Ben Smith objected and, in a meeting with Superintendent Phil Grafton, he gave him a copy of Melissa's letter. The superintendent was disturbed by the contents of the letter, but he chose to ignore it rather than to risk embarrassing and undermining his brother and Kay Molitor by questioning their findings and recommendations. However, in an effort to mollify Ben, he expressed sympathy with "a father's concern for his son," and he urged that "for the love of Joseph," let the "professionals do what is best for him." He also assured Ben that "everything possible would be done" to insure that Joseph was prepared to enter a regular first grade class next year.

Ben refused to accept the superintendent's decision. He met with Melissa in an effort to understand why Joseph fared so well with her and so poorly with Kay Molitor. Melissa detailed for him what she had learned about the operations of the "happy house," how she had temporarily closed it down, and the success she had in working with those children—especially Joseph—who had ben confined to it. Ben shared Melissa's findings with Joseph's psychiatrist, and he discovered they corroborated the stories about the "happy house" that the psychiatrist had heard from several of the children he treated. Armed with this information, Ben filed a formal complaint against Kay Molitor and Bill Grafton with the school-committee chairperson and with the state commissioner of education. The complaint requested an investigation and public hearing into Kay Molitor and Bill Grafton's "questionable classroom practices, faulty testing and referral practices, and failure to comply with P.L. 94–142 requirements." Ben was supported in the complaint by the psychiatrist who acted on behalf of the several children he had treated who were victims of the "happy house."

When Ben filed his complaint, the school committee was in the midst of a power struggle because the untimely death of chairperson John Molitor left his party in tenuous control, and the opposition was organizing to win the spring election. Consequently, when the acting chairperson took over, he was anxious to avoid a controversial issue, such as Ben's complaint, which could result in adverse publicity and prove extremely damaging. On the day he received the complaint, he warned Superintendent Phil Grafton that unless Ben were persuaded to withdraw the complaint, the party could lose control of the school committee and Phil's contract, which was in its final year, would not be renewed. He ordered Phil to resolve the issue quickly so that he would not have to report the complaint at the next school committee meeting which was only ten days away.

Phil met with Kay Molitor and his brother, Bill, that evening and explained why he had to resolve the issue and how he would do it. Neither Kay nor Bill liked his solution, but they had little choice other than to support it. The next morning Phil met with Ben and offered the following five-point compromise if Ben would withdraw the complaint and make no further public comment on it. First, Kay Molitor would close the "happy house" immediately and would retire from teaching at the end of the school year. She would be replaced by Melissa Mitchell who would be given a full-time, tenure-track position. Second, Joseph would remain in the nongraded special education class for the remainder of the school year. He would be assigned Melissa's regular first grade class the following September. Third, Ben would be appointed principal of Coleville West High when the position became vacant at the end of the school year. Fourth, a new position of Associate Director of Testing and Special Education Programs would be created and filled by a specialist in these areas. The

Associate Director would share equally in all decision making with Director Bill Grafton. Fifth, in addition to withdrawing the complaint and making no public comment on it, Ben and his wife would agree not to become involved in any future actions brought by others against Kay Molitor and Bill Grafton.

Phil reminded Ben that if he continued to pursue the complaint, he could not be considered a "team player" and would not be appointed principal of Coleville West High. Further, Phil indicated that he would not be inclined to hire Melissa Mitchell if she remained identified with an issue that sought to disrupt and embarrass the school system. He also noted that an investigation and hearing, would be controversial, divisive, and destructive of faculty morale. Further, it would take months and could prove difficult for Joseph, placing him under considerable stress and complicating his relationship with the other children and teachers. Phil concluded by requiring Ben to give him his decision by the following morning.

That evening Ben and Flora discussed the very difficult decision they would have to make. Should they reject the compromise and pursue the complaint or should they accept the compromise and withdraw the complaint? They must make a decision by the following morning. For the love of Joseph—and/or all other parties involved—what should they do?

# Study Guide for Case #9

To the Instructor and Student::

This guide is designed to assist the student in analyzing this case in the following ways. It suggests:

1. a major *Area of Educational Concern* that is central to the case upon which the student should focus his/her research efforts.

2. *Concepts* that are related to key dimensions of the case and that the student should seek to understand. These *Concepts* have broad implications for educational theory and practice and are listed as *Pivotal Terms.*

3. *Questions* that are concerned with problems raised by the case and that the student use as a resource in researching the case;

Space is provided for students to record *Comments and Additions* on Area of Educational Concern, Concepts, Questions, and Reference Material.

## Case #9
*"For the Love of Joseph"*

1. *Area of Educational Concern:* How much input should parents, physicians and other professionals, and private agencies have in the determination of a student's grade placement, curriculum, and school program?

2. *Concepts-Pivotal Terms:*

| | |
|---|---|
| P.L. 94–142 | single-parent family |
| exceptional child | minority hiring |
| least restrictive environment | learning disability |
| special education program | Montessori method |
| PARC v. Commonwealth (1972) | role model |
| labeling | socialization skills |
| MARC v MD (Mills) 1974 | accountability |
| discrimination | competency |
| Individual Education Plan (IEP) | hyperactivity |
| Multidisciplinary Team (MDT) | educable |

3. *Questions:*

It is possible to have local control of schools without involving partisan politics?

Should schools be required to mainstream exceptional children?

Why have P.L. 94–142 requirements created problems for state and local legislators and educators?

What avenues exist for laypersons (parents or concerned citizens) to appeal school policies they question or oppose?

Who should determine if a child should be mainstreamed?

Should all school personnel be required to attend courses/workshops on working with the handicapped?

What type of limits should be set on a least restrictive environment?

Does least restrictive environment hinder the non-handicapped?

4. *Reference Material:*

Cardell, Cheryl and Rene Pormar. (1988). Teacher perceptions of temperment characteristics of children classified as learning disabled. *Journal of Learning Disabilities* 21(8), 497–501.

Duke, Daniel L. (1986). Understanding what it means to be a teacher. *Educational Leadership,* 44(2), 26–33.

Epstein, Joyce L. (1987). Parent involvement: What research says to administrators. *Education and Urban Society.* 19(2), 119–136.

Feeney, Stephanie and Sysko, Lynda. (1986). Professional ethics in early childhood education: Survey results. *Young Children,* 42(1), 15–20.

Lomatey, Kafi. (1987). Black principals for black students. *Urban Education.* 21(8), 497–501.

National Joint Committee on Learning Disabilities. (1987). Learning disabilities: Issues in the preparation of professional personnel. *Journal of Learning Disabilities,* 20(4), 229–231.

Nelson, Michael C. (1988). Social skills training for handicapped students. *Teaching Exceptional Children,* 88(3), 19–23.

Swanson, H. Lee. (1987). Information processing theory and learning disabilities: An overview. *Journal of Learning Disabilities,* 20(1), 3–7.

# A Matter of Local Choice

Of the numerous islands off the New England coast, Harbour Island had remained an idyllic, picturesque refuge, free of the ravages of pollution, urban sprawl, and overpopulation. Its inhabitants, who engaged chiefly in farming, were direct descendents of the earliest colonists to settle in North America. They took considerable pride in their rich cultural heritage and were anxious to preserve the way of life they had inherited from their forefathers. Consequently, they had made few concessions to the "progress" which affluence and technology had brought to the communities on the mainland that surrounded them. The forty-five minute ferry ride, the only transportation link connecting the Island to the mainland, had further isolated them from the mainstream of changing times and had permitted them to continue their unique lifestyle unchallenged. But all of this was suddenly threatened by the enactment of a law establishing a statewide regionalization program for the schools.

Dr. Harriet Snow, a newly appointed Commissioner of Education, who had jurisdiction over Harbour Island and all of the other areas of the state, had persuaded the state legislature to enact a law requiring consolidation of the existing thirty school districts into six large regional districts. Commissioner Snow's action was based upon recommendations made by the state department of education after an exhaustive study of the state's educational system. The purpose of the law was to eliminate school districts with enrollments of less than 300 pupils and to end "one-room schoolhouses" where children in several grades were taught by the same teacher. The law required: first, the busing of children to those existent centrally-located schools with adequate facilities; and second, the construction of new schools (sixty percent of the cost to be subsidized by state funds) in those central locations that did not have adequate facilities available. The law also required each school district to comply with Public Law 94–142 and provide the facilities, services, and special-education personnel necessary for mainstreaming the handicapped. The thirty school districts were given five years to phase out the operation of "one-room schools" and to incorporate their faculty and student body in a regionalized school district. School districts seeking exemption from the law were given one year to file a petition with the commissioner.

The new law applied directly to small school districts such as Harbour Island where student enrollment never exceeded 250 and where the "one-room schoolhouse" concept was commonly utilized. The Islanders had built a two-story stone building in 1901, and the three large rooms on the first floor were used for kindergarten through grade six while the three large rooms on the second floor housed grades seven through twelve. The building had been maintained in excellent condition, and its facilities included a fine library and a sizable collection of audio-visual aids. The six-member faculty and the superintendent/principal were all graduates of accredited institutions of learning and held advanced certificates of study or masters degrees.

The Islanders were proud of their school and supported its faculty. In turn, Superintendent/Principal Phillip Jason and his faculty sought to mold the schools' operations around the community's needs. The school's hours were structured to allow students sufficient time to complete their daily farm chores before coming to class, and the school's calendar was arranged to permit students to help during the planting and harvesting seasons. Jason ran a tight and orderly school, and his staff was expected to develop a detailed syllabus for each course taught which prescribed specific readings from texts and required homework assignments, class recitations, daily quizzes, and unit and final exams. Teachers demanded preparation, attention and effort from their students, and they summoned parents to school when students failed to comply. The curriculum consisted of prescribed courses in academic areas with a few electives on the secondary level in commercial courses and fine arts. There were no programs in industrial arts and in vocational and business training. Jason had excellent rapport with his staff, was respected by the students, and worked very closely with their parents. He was articulate and during his eleven years as superintendent/principal, he had little difficulty gaining the Islander's endorsement of school budgets that insured his faculty the same salary levels as on the mainland.

The Islander's reaction to the new law was dramatic and immediate. At a heavily attended town meeting, they attacked the law as an infringement on their right ("local control") to determine their children's education. They directed Jason to file an appeal requesting that the Harbour Island school district be allowed to continue to exist independent of the regional school district. Jason drew up a petition in which he addressed three issues. First, he carefully spelled out the success of his school program in meeting the children's educational needs while remaining sensitive to the unique demands of the Island's economy. Second, he warned of the problems that would be created by ferrying students to a centrally located school on the mainland. Finally, he cited the desire of the Islanders to control the educational experience of their children to insure that it would remain firmly rooted in the tradition and culture they cherished.

When Commissioner Snow received the petition, she found herself confronted with a difficult decision. The state department study offered strong arguments for allowing no exceptions to the regionalization plan. The economies and efficiency realized by the larger school districts would mean modern comprehensive schools with student-teacher ratios of less than twenty-five to one. On the elementary level, specialists would be employed to develop programs for the artistic and creative child, for the exceptional child, and for the child with learning disabilities. On the secondary level, a diversified curriculum would be developed with programs in classical studies, business training, shop and vocational skills, home economics, and industrial and fine arts. Students would have the opportunity to participate in competitive sports, band, work/study programs, and consumer education training. Since regionalization would make the schools eligible for state and federal funds, they would receive the most recent developments in educational technology and training for programs in teaching the basics as well as the more advanced courses in sciences, languages, and maths. Finally, at all grade levels schools would comply with Public Law 94–142 by providing facilities, services, and specially trained personnel to comply with the mainstreaming requirements.

The arguments for not incorporating Harbour Island into the regional district were equally persuasive. Harbour Island students had performed well on tests administered by the state department of education. Students on the elementary level had scored higher than mainland students in reading and math while secondary students had scored higher on achievement tests in science, literature, and history. Currently there were no handicapped students in the school population; therefore, there was not problem of failing to comply with Public Law 94–142 requirements. There were problems in ferrying and busing the Island children to the mainland school The trip would take at least one hour under ideal conditions and could be considerably longer in the winter when ferry runs were delayed by the weather. Students would be required to leave for school early in the morning and would not arrive home until late in the afternoon. This extended school day would impose an economic hardship on the families who relied upon their children to help on the farm before and after school hours. Finally, the Islanders expressed suspicion and hostility toward what they viewed as an open, elective curriculum and an unstructured, permissive, "fads and frills" approach to education. They did not believe that large classes with two or more grades taught by the same teacher had adversely affected their children's education. They were convinced that they should have a direct voice in how their children would be educated, and they threatened to obstruct the regionalization process through the courts and in the legislature.

Commissioner Snow carefully weighed the arguments advanced by both sides. She favored regionalization but was also sympathetic to the unique circumstances of the Harbour Islanders. She was anxious to avoid the long legal fight that would result if the Islanders went to court. On the other hand she knew that if she granted the petition, other districts, seeking to retain "local control," would also request exemption. She must decide what is best for the students, for the state, and for the particular communities. What should she do? Should she deny the petition and incorporate Harbour Island into the regional district or should she grant an exemption and allow Harbour Island to remain outside the regional district?

# Study Guide for Case #10

To the Instructor and Student::

This guide is designed to assist the student in analyzing this case in the following ways. It suggests:

1. a major *Area of Educational Concern* that is central to the case and upon which the student should focus his/her research efforts.

2. *Concepts* that are related to key dimensions of the case and that the student should seek to understand. These *Concepts* have broad implications for educational theory and practice and are listed as *Pivotal Terms.*

3. *Questions* that are concerned with problems raised by the case and that the student should explore further for possible issues;

4. *Reference Material* that is related to the case and that the student should use as a resource in researching the case;

## Case #10

*"A Matter of Local Choice"*

1. *Area of Educational Concern:* Who should determine the what (curriculum), the where (location), and the how (methodology) of our children's educational experience?

2. *Concepts-Pivotal Terms:*

| | |
|---|---|
| "one-room schoolhouse" | social mobility |
| traditional/prescribed curriculum | regionalization |
| comprehensive/elective curriculum | busing |
| cultural diversity | mainstreaming |
| local control | state aid/state control |
| decentralization | cosmopolitan |
| provincial | cultural heritage |
| extra curricular activities | professional standards |
| teacher-pupil ratio | community standards |
| Tenth Amendment | Public Law 94–142 |
| educational technology | exemption |

3. *Questions:*

How responsive should an education program be to the local community's needs and concern?

Should schools provide programs directed at industrial, vocational and business training?

What are the advantages and disadvantages of the state determining educational policy?

What are the advantages and disadvantages of the local community determining educational policy?

Does the "one-room schoolhouse" provide an experience that has educational worth?

Should local communities expect schools to promote the relationships, loyalties, and values peculiar to their geographic area?

Should students have the same teacher for more than one year and for different subjects?

What are the advantages/disadvantages of a curriculum of prescribed academic courses with few electives in other areas?

4. *Reference Material:*

Anrig, G. (1985). The decentralization controversy. *The Education Digest,* 51(11), 125–127.

Archer, Chalmers Jr. (1985). Needed: A one educational system. *Education,* 105(3), 323–326.

Baldwin, Robert E. (1982). Freedom of choice in education. *American Education,* 18(7), 17–23.

Bussard, Ellen. (1982). Strategies for consideration when closing a school. *The Education Digest,* 47(5), 9–12.

Heyns, Roger W. (1984). Education and society: A complex interaction. *American Education,* 20(4), 2–5.

Rogers, David. (1982). School decentralization: It works. *Social Policy,* 12(4), 13–23.

Turnbull, Brenda J. (1985). Using governance and support systems to advance school improvements. *The Elementary School Journal,* 85(3), 337–351.

# The Dark Lady in the Blue Sari

Mary Ellen Bentley, the chairperson of the math department at Railyn Classical High, was prim, proper, and prepared. She tolerated no nonsense from the students, demanded much of them, expected total commitment from them, hoped high for them, and, when problems arose, was willing to meet them half way. She was a sensitive, concerned, conscientious teacher and administrator respected by faculty and students and supported by parents.

Mary Ellen was not married and lived with her parents. She felt deeply indebted to them for the considerable sacrifices they had made for her. She had been a menopausal baby whose birth had left her mother crippled with a serious heart ailment which caused chronic bouts of pain. Her parents were low-paid unskilled factory workers who had endured the hardships of poverty to insure that she completed her college education. Mary Ellen knew what deprivation meant, and she was painfully aware of the sacrifices parents make for the welfare and advancement of their children. These lessons were not lost in her relations with students, faculty, and parents; she remained particularly sensitive and highly responsive to the needy and to those who sacrificed for them.

Railyn Classical High was often referred to as the "poor child's key to college." It was located in the ghetto area of Railyn, a large city that suffered heavy unemployment when it smokestack industries were closed by their failure to modernize to meet foreign competition. Though the shrinking tax-base and the flight of the professional middle class to suburban areas had reduced Railyn to the poorest school district in the state, its Classical High remained a center of academic excellence whose graduates easily gained admission to the finest higher institutions of learning in the region and frequently were awarded scholarships and other forms of financial assistance. Many parents of low-income families viewed Classical High as the only opportunity for their children to attain the education that would enable them to realize a better life. They were particularly anxious for their children to attend, and they were willing to make any sacrifice to allow them the opportunity to complete their schooling.

The strength and success of Classical High's math department rested in the faculty's excellent academic training, in their singleness of purpose in demanding homework, effort, and preparation from all their students, and in their requiring of a highly structured curriculum that forced all students through a tight-knit sequence of computer and math courses from the introductory to the advanced levels. Math department faculty took pride in the quality of preparation their students received. They attributed their success to their ability to work together effectively as a team while at the same time making specific contributions as individuals in their areas of expertise. The friendships among the math faculty extended beyond the classroom. All of them had been hired within the past fifteen years and strong ties had developed as they matured, shared, and experienced together the problems and issues of a common workplace. It was, therefore, a matter of grave concern for them when they learned in the last month of the summer recess that one of their colleagues, Alice Golden, had been stricken by cancer. She would be on sick leave for one-half the school year, but she probably would never return to teaching.

Mary Ellen moved quickly to find a long-term substitute replacement who could effectively cover Alice's classes for the present and who could also be considered a viable candidate if the position had to be filled on a permanent basis in the future. Because of the need to fill the position within three weeks, the superintendent allowed her to select a substitute without deferring to a screening committee. Mary Ellen chose Nihla Shanumbara, a doctoral candidate in mathematics at the state university, who was certified to teach on the secondary level and who had taught math in a private school. Nihla had excellent credentials. She had earned A's in all her graduate level courses in math and computer science, and she had received a high recommendation on her teaching effectiveness from the headmaster of the private school where she had taught.

Nihla needed the job. She had come to America with her husband from a far eastern country seven years previously. They had been granted a visa because of her husband's work as an engineer in a robotics laboratory. During her first two years in America, Nihla, who had earned an undergraduate math degree in her native country, completed a Master of Art degree in teaching.She also taught at a private school until the seventh month of her pregnancy. Shortly after the birth of her daughter, Nihla learned that her husband had multiple sclerosis, that he would be unable to continue to work, and, consequently, that his visa would no longer be valid. Nihla immediately enrolled in a doctoral program, and as a graduate student, she was granted a visa that allowed her husband and child to remain with her in America.

Nihla's graduate work progressed slowly because she carried a reduced course-load in order to work to support her family. This caused emigration officials to question her graduate student status and to delay acting on her request for an extension of her visa. However, her visa was quickly renewed with her appointment to the Railyn school system. Nihla came to view this teaching position as critical to her very survival, providing a badly needed income and securing her visa. Shortly after being hired, she confessed to Mary Ellen that she was anxious to prove her competency as a teacher so that she would be retained if Alice Golden did not return.

Mary Ellen assigned Nihla five classes to teach: two freshman geometry classes, two sophomore classes in computer science, and a senior honors class in calculus. The chairperson usually taught the honors course, but she wanted to balance Nihla's schedule with bright, mature students and a more challenging advanced course. On the Friday afternoon of the week before classes began, she met with Nihla and explained the school and departmental policies, defined course requirements, and provided her with several texts and a large quantity of other materials relating to her assigned courses. Mary Ellen noted that when she sought to help Nihla carry these materials, Nihla refused her assistance even though she was obviously tired and overburdened. Mary Ellen also noted that when they were moving from room to room, Nihla, despite all she was carrying, always moved quickly ahead and held the door open for her. From Nihla's brief comments during these incidents, Mary Ellen became aware of a major cultural difference separating the two women. Nihla spoke of carefully observing "levels of difference," "recognizing her inferior place" in relation to administrators who were "above her" and expecting students to "recognize their inferior place" in relation to teachers who were "above them."

When Nihla left school that day, she forgot her handbag in the chairperson's office, so Mary Ellen, on her way home, dropped it off at Nihla's apartment. Nihla lived in the poorest section of the city, and though her flat was clean, it was sparsely furnished and badly in need of repair. She showed Mary Ellen her baby and then introduced her husband. Mary Ellen was moved to considerable pity by his physical condition. He lay helplessly on a couch suffering from the loss of muscular coordination and from speech defects characteristic of the advancing stages of multiple sclerosis.

During the first several weeks of school, Mary Ellen met regularly with Nihla to discuss her classes. She found Nihla to be organized, knowledgeable, and to have carefully prepared her lessons and homework assignments. She sought to befriend Nihla as a colleague and to encourage her to share any problems that should arise in class. But Nihla, reflecting a different cultural perspective, rejected her appeal. Rather, she saw Mary Ellen as "two persons"—an administrator and a teacher—and she responded to each person differently. As the administrator, Mary Ellen was above her; Mary Ellen's directives were "never to be questioned," and her authority must "always be respected." As the teacher, Mary Ellen was equal to her; it would be "inexcusable" for Mary Ellen to handle Nihla's classroom problems, and it would be an "admission of failure" on Nihla's part to ask for help. Mary Ellen sought to dissuade Nihla by arguing that she hoped "Nihla would help her" if she had a problem, but it was to no avail.

The principal of Railyn Classical High was Joseph Bennett. He enjoyed the longest tenure of any administrator in the history of the school, and his success as an administrator was marked by three practices. First, he maintained a rigid chain of command that held each level within the hierarchy completely responsible for its decisions. This allowed him to "share the praise" when things went right and to "finger the guilty" when things went wrong. Second, he closely monitored all school activities and reserved for himself the final decision on anything he perceived to be controversial and that might bring public disfavor upon the school. This allowed him to intervene, and to control unilaterally, the operations of the school whenever he felt it was necessary. And, third, he maintained an "open office door policy" welcoming faculty and students at any time to discuss school affairs. This allowed him to remain tuned in to the gossip of the school and to play individuals, interests, and factions off one another in a leadership game of divide and rule. It also allowed him to establish an extraordinary rapport with the student body; students responded to his congeniality and availability by frequently stopping at his office to chat and joke.

It was during these informal discussions with students that Bennett learned of their reaction to the new math teacher, "the dark lady in the blue sari." They felt she was "in love with math," and seemed to "know everything about it," but they found her classes "boring" and admitted they did not always pay attention. They felt that while her "accent" and the "lilt" to her voice were appealing, she was "cold, severe, and unfriendly." They admitted they were noisy in class, but they resented her referring to them as "rude, ignorant, lazy Americans" when she became angry.

Mary Ellen learned of the problems in Nihla's math classes after the first quarter marking-period ended in November. The counselor for the senior class informed her that several of the best students in the calculus class were failing and that twenty-one of the twenty-four students in the class had complained about Nihla's teaching. He reminded her that these were the same honors students who had done so well the previous year in Mary Ellen's algebra class. He suggested that the very nature of the complaints and the number of quality, math students involved demanded that she intervene and resolve whatever the problem was. He noted that she was highly respected by these students and that many of them had asked to meet with her.

Mary Ellen invited the students in the calculus class to an "unofficial" meeting after school hours where they would have the opportunity to "air their feelings." She asked the guidance teacher to attend and to take notes on all that was said. At the meeting she began by telling the twenty-one students who attended that Mrs. Shanumbara would be given a copy of the notes taken but that their names would not be revealed. She then conducted the meeting in an absolutely impartial manner, avoiding any comments for or against teacher or student and not giving any indication of approval or disapproval to what was being said. At the close of the meeting, she thanked the students, asserted she would look into what had been said, and promised to get back to them soon.

When Mary Ellen gave Nihla a copy of the notes taken at the meeting, Nihla expressed shock and dismay. She felt that students had "no right" to question her and to "involve another teacher;" rather, she alone should have been confronted with all complaints related to her teaching and classroom practices. She reminded Mary Ellen that she viewed it as an admission of failure when a teacher allowed another teacher to handle her classroom problems. Then, she sadly observed: "You have taken away my pride from me as a teacher." Mary Ellen disagreed and emphasized that she was "seeking to understand why students were performing so poorly" and "not trying to discredit anyone." She was concerned that the students involved, all of whom were college-bound, profit from the calculus course and retain their excellent scholastic records. She proposed that she visit the class for the next two weeks and that they meet after each class to discuss her observations. Nihla reluctantly agreed but only after bitterly commenting: "The students have been out to destroy me, and now they have done it with your help."

Mary Ellen informed the principal of the problems in the calculus class and of her planned visits. He told her of the unfavorable feedback he had received from the students on all Nihla's classes and warned that if parents of the honors students complained, he would intervene. While he endorsed Mary Ellen's plan, he clearly indicated that he would not tolerate "boat-rockers" and that the "dark lady in the blue sari" would be "quickly shipped out" if she did not "shape up."

Mary Ellen held another "unofficial" meeting with the calculus class to explain the purpose of her visits. It was an "attempt to understand the problem so that it could be resolved." It was not a "witch hunt" designed to place either student or teacher "on trial or to affix blame." She told the students that she held them responsible for noise and disruptions in class and that she expected them to "straighten out their behavior" and "present no further disciplinary issues."

In both her class visits and in her discussions of her observations with Nihla, Mary Ellen discovered that while the students' complaints were not without foundation, they were also a result of misunderstanding. There were three major complaints. First, students claimed that the teacher "does not know what she is doing" and "does not understand our questions." But Mary Ellen found that Nihla had a superb mastery of her subject matter, clearly understood questions asked, and sought to present thorough, detailed answers. Unfortunately, her teaching strategy was ineffective. She would answer specific questions directed at a particular step in a problem by returning to the beginning of the problem and carefully retracing all the steps. This proved to be a tedious and distracting process, and students often were no longer paying attention by the time she discussed their specific area of confusion. Also, this process was extremely time-consuming; consequently, Nihla was unable to cover the course material required in the syllabus.

The second student complaint was that the teacher "is boring and unfriendly and her classes are dull." Mary Ellen found that Nihla's insistence upon a classroom environment that was sterile, formal, and impersonal, and her failure to interact with the students in a more open, familiar fashion, reflected her cultural beliefs in levels of difference. Nihla viewed her place as being above the students, and she expected them to recognize and accept their place below her. They were to be "polite, prepared, attentive, and seek to emulate her love of acknowledge." Her job was "strictly teaching" and "not befriending, entertaining, socializing, or identifying closely with students."

The third student complaint was that the teacher "is unable to control the class" and "makes cruel and upsetting comments." Students admitted classes were noisy because they had "fooled around." But while they regretted their behavior, they also expressed considerable resentment that Nihla referred to them as "bad, ill-mannered, spoiled Americans" who were "ruining her life", "ripping the flesh" from her heart, "destroying her livelihood", and "taking away money needed for her husband". Mary Ellen found that Nihla's inability to control the class resulted from her being new to the system, not totally familiar with rules and procedures, and, therefore, hesitant to send students to the office who were noisy, late, or cutting classes. When students took advantage of her failure to discipline them and did not automatically show the respect she expected, Nihla felt their behavior was reprehensible and chastized them verbally. Further, her highly emotional comments, which students found "upsetting," reflected the heavy personal burden she labored under. She was working full time as a teacher, studying part-time as a graduate student, maintaining a household, and caring for a baby and a sick husband. When students misbehaved and were not responsive in class, she feared it could lead to her losing her teaching position. This would have catastrophic consequences for her; it would leave her without income to support her family, with problems in renewing her visa, and with little opportunity to complete her doctoral degree. Thus, Mary Ellen understood why Nihla cried out to her noisy students that their behavior was "ruining her life, ripping her flesh", etc.

By the end of her visits, Mary Ellen had become painfully aware of the cultural differences and personal problems that explained so much of Nihla's teaching and disciplining shortcomings. She felt sorry for her, but she was appalled by how poorly the class had fared because of Nihla's ineffectiveness. She was concerned at the failure of the class to cover the required material, and she was disturbed by how badly confused several of the brighter students had become. She felt that Nihla must set aside cultural differences and personal problems, and she must change her approach to teaching. To insure the latter occurred, she gave Nihla the following three-part directive. First, Nihla must stop giving detailed repetitious answers; rather, she must address specific student questions with clear, succinct answers. She would be expected to use class time effectively and to cover all material required in the syllabus. Second, she must implement all school policies and procedures such as taking attendance, assigning late students to detention, etc. She would be expected to control the class and avoid noise and disruptions. And third, she must stop making personal and pejorative comments to students; rude or disruptive students must be sent to the vice-principal's office to be disciplined. She would be expected to earn the respect of the students, demanding it through her teaching effectiveness and a firm-but-fair approach to disciplining. Mary Ellen also informed Nihla that she would be visiting her classes at least once a week to insure the directive was followed. She would also meet regularly with her after school to discuss classroom management, school policies, and instructional techniques.

During the next school quarter, Mary Ellen was pleasantly surprised by the complete turnabout in Nihla's teaching performance and classroom management. Nihla closely adhered to the directive, addressing student questions effectively, covering required material fully, and handling discipline problems adequately. Unfortunately, these improvements came too late for some students. Four of the brighter ones, who had received F in calculus for the first quarter, had to drop the course mid-way into the second quarter. They had fallen too far behind in their understanding of the material during the poorly conducted classes of the first quarter and were so hopelessly confused that they were unable to benefit from the improved learning environment of the second quarter. Mary Ellen was greatly troubled by this turn of events. She realized that these students, whose low-income parents had made untold sacrifices to keep them in school, had seriously blemished their scholastic records and, in turn, had greatly diminished their opportunities for admission to college and for scholarship aid.

In general, students responded favorably to Nihla's classes throughout the second quarter, and Mary Ellen and Principal Bennett received positive feedback from them. They felt "the dark lady in the blue sari" was not the most "exciting" teacher they had; but she did "know her math," and they felt they "learned a lot" in her classes. They wished she would "smile" and be "more friendly," but they felt she was "patient" and "gave help" when asked. While Mary Ellen was pleased with these reports, she also recognized that Nihla continued to embrace a cultural outlook that was in opposition to values and practices that were central to the American public school experience. In their after school meetings and discussions, Nihla remained adamant in professing her beliefs in levels of difference, in respect being owed and not earned, in recognizing and accepting one's place, in always deferring to authority, etc. Consequently, Mary Ellen remained apprehensive that Nihla would reflect these views again in future classroom practices and create new teaching and disciplining problems.

On the Friday before the end of the second quarter, Principal Bennett informed Mary Ellen that Alice Golden would not return to teaching and that a permanent replacement for the position must be found. He said he would consider Nihla for the position only if Mary Ellen recommended her; however, he would hold Mary Ellen accountable for Nihla's continuing adjustment, development, and improvement as a teacher. He expressed considerable ambivalence concerning the retention of Nihla. He recognized that she had a superb math background, and he knew, with math teachers in short supply, it would be difficult to recruit anyone equally qualified. But he remained concerned with the problems she had initially controlling her classes, with her cold personality, and with her distant attitude toward her students. However, he was pleased with recent student reports of her improvement and effectiveness as a teacher, and he felt she "appeared to be turning things around." He gave Mary Ellen the weekend to make a decision; he planned to launch an early recruitment effort for a math teacher if Nihla was not selected.

Over the weekend Mary Ellen carefully considered the very difficult decision she had to make. Should she recommend that Nihla be appointed to the position or should she recommend that Nihla not be retained as a teacher? What should she do?

# Study Guide for Case #11

To the Instructor and Student:

This guide is designed to assist the student in analyzing this case in the following ways. It suggests:

1.  a major *Area of Educational Concern* that is central to the case and upon which the student should focus his/her research efforts.

2.  *Concepts* that are related to key dimensions of the case and that the student should seek to understand. These *Concepts* have broad implications for educational theory and practice and are listed as *Pivotal Terms*.

3.  *Questions* that are concerned with problems raised by the case and that the student should explore further for possible issues;

4.  *Reference Material* that is related to the case and that the student should use as a resource in researching the case;

## Case #11

*"The Dark Lady in the Blue Sari"*

1.  *Area of Educational Concern:* What role should cultural pluralism play in the American educational enterprise?

2  *Concepts-Pivotal Terms:*

| | |
|---|---|
| cultural pluralism | inner-city school |
| acculturation | classroom management |
| teacher competency | prescribed curriculum |
| social norms | socialization |
| xenophobia | affirmative action |
| language barrier | culture shock |
| cultural relativism | racism |
| cultural diversity | cultural bias |
| teacher accountability | probationary period |
| ethnocentrism | teacher certification |
| teaching strategy/methodology | long-term substitute |

3. *Questions:*

Should students be involved in teacher evaluation?

Who should be responsible for supervising first year teachers?

What should be the nature of teacher-pupil interaction if effective classroom management is to be realized?

What should be the nature of administrator-teacher interaction if teachers are to be responsible for, committed to, and supportive of school policies and procedures?

Why do students tend to take advantage of foreign teachers as they do with substitute teachers?

To what extent is affirmative action applicable to schools in today's pluralistic society?

How can the school effectively promote cultural relativism?

How can the schools help the first year teacher meet the demands of classroom management and develop effective teaching methods?

4. *Reference Material:*

Blumberg, Arthur and Jones R. Stevan. (1987). The teacher's control over supervision. *Educational Leadership,* 44(8), 59–62.

Dela-Dora Delmo. (1987). Quality supervision and organization for quality teaching. *Educational Leadership,* 44(8), 35–38.

Hawthorne, Rebecca K. (1986). The professional teacher's dilemma: Balancing autonomy and obligation. *Educational Leadership,* 44(2), 34–35.

Henry, Marvin A. (1986). Strengths and needs of first-year teachers. *The Teacher Educator,* 22(2), 10–18.

Presmeg, Norma C. (1988). School mathematics in culture-conflict situations. *Educational Studies in Mathematics,* 19(2), 163–177.

Simon, Martin A. (1986). The teacher's role in increasing student understanding of mathematics. *Educational Leadership,* 43(7), 40–43.

Singh, B. R. (1988). Cognitive styles: Cultural pluralism and effective teaching and learning. *International Review of Education, 39*(3), 355–370.

# Who Shall Teach Our Children?

When Doctor Jonathan Crabbe was appointed Associate Professor of Oceanography at West Coast College, his wife Trudy was particularly concerned about the quality of the school system her son and two daughters would attend. West Coast College was located in a semi-rural beach resort area thirty miles from a large city, and those of its residents who did not work at the College, operated small shops or commuted to jobs in the city. Several faculty members' wives taught at the schools, and Trudy had learned, during her husband's interviews, that a generous school budget supported relatively new buildings, equipped with the latest facilities educational technology could provide, and staffed by a highly paid faculty.

Trudy's interest in the quality of education her children received emanated from her own training and experiences. Prior to the birth of her first child, she had taught English in a public high school for three years, and she had also served for three years as a Peace Corps volunteer in a Central American country. In her work with the Peace Corps, she had successfully established and operated the first high school in the area, and her account of how this was achieved had been published in a national educational journal.

When the Crabbes arrived at West Coast College, their twin daughters were twelve years old and their son was ten. The daughters were enrolled in a junior high school, and the son entered an elementary school. Trudy joined the Parent Teacher Association and quickly assumed a leadership role. She showed slides and lectured on her Peace Corps experiences, and she headed several committees to promote cooperation and interest in the schools. She became popular with the parents, was respected by the teachers, and within two years she ran as an unendorsed candidate for the school committee and won by a large majority.

Trudy believed that to be an effective member of the school committee she should become thoroughly acquainted with the operations of the schools. She began by making a number of unannounced visits to the high school where she observed the teachers at work. She was deeply disturbed by what she saw and did not always hide her dismay. She felt that many of the teachers were either lazy or grossly incompetent, that the school was poorly administered, and that the curriculum was unsound and encouraged poor teaching practices.

She noted that the biology teacher did not use a text and based his course on mimeographed outlines that were often simplistic and inaccurate, that the chairman of the history department usually arrived ten minutes late for his classes, that two of the math teachers were sloppy in grading tests and tardy in returning them, that two of the English teachers did not correct spelling, grammar or syntactical construction on compositions submitted by the children, and that the Spanish teacher was frequently unprepared for class.

She felt that discipline was poorly handled because the vice principal, who was responsible for disciplining students, was too permissive and rarely placed a student on detention or summoned a parent to school. She felt that students ignored his fatherly lectures and admonitions and that teachers recognized the futility of sending discipline problems to him and allowed students to continue their infractions of the rules provided they did not reduce the classrooms to outright chaos. She felt that the incidents of fistfighting, bullying, and shouting obscenities occurred too frequently in the corridors and lunchroom and that the school plant suffered too high a rate of property destruction from vandalism.

Trudy also questioned the curriculum the school followed and the teaching strategies adopted by the faculty. The curriculum did not consist of the traditional full-year courses in history, math, English, etc.; rather, students could select four ''nine-week mini-courses'' in each of these subject matter areas. These offerings varied from ''Chaucer'' to ''Sport Stories'' and from ''Roman History'' to the ''History of the Radio.'' The teachers were divided in their approaches to teaching these courses. Some found nine weeks to be too brief a term for assigning lengthy papers and requiring essay exams, and they tended to evaluate students on the basis of weekly multiple choice tests and short papers. Others followed an independent study format in which students decided upon a topic and were responsible for selecting the readings and completing a project paper. These projects often involved community resources, and students spent considerable time away from school and classroom supervision. Trudy felt both of these teaching strategies were poor. The former because it did not allow for term papers and essay exams, and the latter because it was not sufficiently structured and did not allow for adequate teacher supervision of field experiences.

Trudy expressed her reservations concerning the high school to the principal, but while he listened respectfully, he tended to dismiss them on the grounds that "her philosophy of education was more traditional," and that she was blinded to the advantages and soundness of a "more progressive approach to education." The principal felt it was "unfair" of her to criticize his teachers since she had not taught for more than ten years and was not "familiar with this generation of children and the best way to teach them." He warned that her unannounced visits to the classroom were "destroying teacher morale" and that several teachers had complained she was "disrupting classes." He asked that she not visit classes again unless she received the teacher's permission in advance.

At the following school committee meeting, Trudy reported her observations of the high school and her conversation with the principal. She expected the committee to investigate her findings and to take action to improve the high school, but instead the members of the committee tended to support the principal they had appointed and the faculty that many of them had been friendly with socially over the years. The committee was also anxious to avoid a confrontation with the teachers' union and a lengthy, controversial, and costly court action which would result from any attempt to reprimand or remove tenured teachers on the grounds of incompetency. In effect, Trudy was told that the "community was satisfied with the operation of the high school" and that she must learn to "accommodate her views to the legal, political, social, and economic realities that confront the committee."

That evening Trudy discussed the committee's decision with her husband. They both agreed that they did not want their twin daughters to enter the high school next year. They realized that they could not afford the tuition fees and transportation costs that would be involved in sending their children to schools in the city. And since there were no other schools available, they decided to withdraw their children from school at the end of the school year and teach them at home.

The following fall, Trudy set up school at home for her three children. She taught three hours of classes in English, Social Studies and Spanish, while her husband taught two hours of classes in the sciences and maths. A sixth hour was devoted to reading and discussing works from the Great Books series.

The Crabbe's school proved quite controversial. The school committee publicly demanded her resignation, and those faculty whose wives taught in the school system severed all social relations with the Crabbes and prohibited their children from playing with the Crabbe children. Trudy wrote a letter to the editor of the local newspaper explaining her reservations concerning the high school and defining the educational experience her children were having at home. She emphasized that her action had been "triggered" by the "failure of the school committee and high school principal to make desperately needed reforms in the school." A flurry of letters followed that either supported or attacked the Crabbes. Some sympathized with the Crabbe's genuine concern for the education of their children; others felt their actions were "disruptive to the school's operations, demeaning to the school's professional staff," and in general, "undermining the public school system."

Several weeks after the Crabbes had set up their school, they received a notice from the superintendent's office that their children were truant and must report to school on the following Monday. They were reminded of the state compulsory school attendance law which required attendance at state certified schools that met the academic standards (curricula, teaching certification, assessment, etc.) for regional accreditation and that complied with the building codes and safety requirements established by state law. They were warned that if they failed to obey this law they could be viewed as "negligent parents" contributing to the "delinquency of minors" and that court action could be taken to declare their children "wards of the state."

The Crabbes responded by consulting a lawyer sympathetic to their cause. They planned to appeal the superintendent's action and to request exception from the law. However, the lawyer warned them that this was a "relatively untested area" of the law, and they could become involved in a long and expensive court action which "could go either way."

On the Sunday evening before their children were required to return to the public schools, Jonathan and Trudy Crabbe held a final conference on the future of their school. They remained totally dissatisfied with the operation of the high school and questioned the quality of education their children would receive. They were quite satisfied with the educational results of the first seven weeks of their school, and their children appeared to enjoy the experience and wanted it to continue. Yet they knew that a long court battle could destroy them financially, and they were uncertain as to the effects the continued controversy and social isolation would have on their children.

The Crabbes were confronted with a difficult decision. Should they stop teaching their children at home and send them to a the local public schools or should they continue their home schooling program? The Crabbes must make their decision by the following day. What should they do?

# Study Guide for Case #12

To the Instructor and Student:

This guide is designed to assist the student in analyzing this case in the following ways. It suggests:

1. a major *Area of Educational Concern* that is central to the case and upon which the student should focus his/her research efforts.

2. *Concepts* that are related to key dimensions of the case and that the student should seek to understand. These *Concepts* have broad implications for educational theory and practice and are listed as *Pivotal Terms*.

3. *Questions* that are concerned with problems raised by the case and that the student should explore further for possible issues;

4. *Reference Material* that is related to the case and that the student should use as a resource in researching the case;

## Case #12

*"Who Shall Teach Our Children?"*

1. *Area of Educational Concern:* Should home schooling be supported by the community and allowed as a viable alternative option to public and private schools?

2. *Concepts-Pivotal Terms:*

| | |
|---|---|
| accountability | teacher competency |
| school committee | prescribed curriculum |
| home schooling | elective courses |
| school attendance law | voucher |
| socialization | Great Books series |
| Peace Corps | school committee |
| Parent Teacher Association | tenure |
| classroom observations | perennialism |
| Pierce v. Soc. of Sisters (1925) | progressivism |
| teacher morale | Wisconsin v. Yodder (1972) |
| alienation | permissiveness |

3. *Questions:*

What should be the nature of the school committee's involvement in the operations of the schools?

Should classes in session be open to observation by the public at any time and without providing advance notice to the teachers?

What recourse do parents have, other than removing their children, when they are dissatisfied with the teachers or programs at a school?

Should parents be given some form of tuition allotment that would enable them to enroll their children in the school of their choice?

Are home school children subject to alienation from their peers?

Who should regulate home schooling?

Can the home schooling movement undermine public school education?

What are the weaknesses and strengths of home schooling?

4. *Reference Material:*

Adelson, Joseph. (1981). What happened to the schools? *Commentary,* 71(3), 36–41.

Divoky, Diane. (1983). The new pioneers of the home-schooling movement. *Phi Delta Kappan,* 64(6), 395–398.

Holt, John. (1983). Schools and home schoolers: A fruitful partnership. *Phi Delta Kappan,* 64(6), 391–394.

Keim, Albert N. (1975). *Compulsory Education and the Amish.* Boston: Beacon Press.

Keisling, Phil. (1982). How to save the public schools. *The New Republic,* 187(17), 27–32.

Konnert, William and Josef Wendel. (1988). Here's what your board should know when asked about home schooling. *The American School Board Journal,* 175(5), 43–44.

Leiberman, Myron. (1986). *Beyond Public Education.* New York: Praeger.

Wade, Theodore E. Jr. (1986). *The Home School Manual.* Auburn, CA: Gazelle Publications.

# The Deal

Harlan Tone had done his graduate work under E. L. Thorndike, and his research showed such promise that he was invited by Columbia University to continue post-doctoral studies in their psychology department. But Tone chose instead to join the staff of Meridith University, a "fringe" Ivy League type institution located in the midwest. Meridith was noted for its excellent psychology program which was staffed by several outstanding scholars in the field.

Tone fit well in the Meridith academic setting. He continued his research and over the next twenty years wrote two books and fifteen articles on his findings. At the age of fifty Tone had become a scholar of national repute who was referred to as *the* authority in his area of research and who was frequently invited to present papers at major conventions. It was not unexpected when, after the retirement of several of his distinguished colleagues, he was appointed chairperson of the psychology department. His appointment did raise questions among several of the younger departmental members who felt his writings had become dated and his research had been "reduced to a nonproductive reworking of old ideas."

Over the next ten years the question of the scholarly value of Tone's research and writings became a major issue in the psychology department. Tone's failure to find a publisher for a manuscript and the rejection of his articles by several refereed professional journals seemed to confirm the criticisms directed at his work by a growing number of his colleagues. Tone's teaching and course offerings also came under attack. Student evaluations of his courses found his teaching style to be "pedantic," his attitude to be "overbearing and authoritarian" and his course content to be a "slavish repetition of the required text and readings."

Tone sought to ignore his critics and to remain as chairperson, but the university administration intervened when two of the younger and most promising scholars in the department threatened to leave unless Tone were removed from his post. The administration found itself in a difficult position because many of the older faculty sympathized with Tone whom they felt had "contributed much in his youth only to be cast aside when he grew older." Tone recognized the vulnerability of the administration's position and forced it to make a deal with him. He agreed to step down as chairperson of the psychology department but only after he was appointed chairperson of the fledgling education department with sufficient funding allocated for the education department to offer graduate degrees at the master and doctoral levels in education.

During his first four years with the education department, Tone developed a master of arts in teaching program with sixty teacher candidates seeking certification at the elementary and secondary levels. He also established a doctoral program in counseling with twelve candidates at various levels of completion of degree requirements. Tone had managed to do all this with a department consisting of only three members besides himself: a full professor of counseling, an assistant professor of school administration and an instructor of educational psychology. Not one member of the department had any experience teaching at the elementary or secondary levels nor was anyone qualified or trained to teach methods courses or to supervise student teachers. Tone had sought to meet this deficiency with retired teachers who were hired as special instructors on a part-time basis, but the use of such staff was severely criticized by the American Association of University Professors (AAUP), the faculty's bargaining unit. To avoid conflict with the AAUP, the administration provided Tone with a tenure-track position at the assistant professor level to be filled by a specialist in the are of methods and student teaching supervision.

Tone filled the position with Mike Sasso, a former high school teacher, who had completed a Ph.D. in philosophy of education. Sasso had been an assistant professor for three years at a teachers' college in California where he headed an undergraduate student teacher program. He had originally come from New England, and he and his family were anxious to return; he viewed Meridith as a step—geographically and professionally—toward home. Tone had selected Sasso from among the many applicants for the position because of his excellent credentials and his enthusiasm for teaching in a graduate program.

122

Tone was pleased when Sasso arrived on campus two months before classes began and volunteered to establish a curriculum resource center. Using a graduate student, and limiting expenses to the cost of postage and university stationary, Sasso converted an abandoned supply room into a resource center filled with texts, journals, monographs, videos, etc. contributed by publishing companies and local businesses and supported by a small grant from a national foundation. During these weeks following his arrival, Sasso also sought to become acquainted with his colleagues at Meridith and the professionals in the public schools with whom he would be associated or working. He approached the chairperson of the philosophy department and arranged to have his philosophy of education course, which would be offered in the fall, cross-listed and credited as a philosophy course as well. He also visited schools where student teachers might be placed and introduced himself to the principals.

Two weeks before the fall semester began, Tone invited Sasso and his wife, Deidre, for dinner. Tone used the occasion to explain how he ran his department and the loyalty he expected from all its members—including their mates. Sasso sat in stunned silence as Tone reprimanded him for "making deals" with the philosophy department without first consulting with him and for visiting schools without first obtaining his permission. Deidre stared at the floor in disbelief as Tone noted that he expected wives to speak only favorably of the department or not at all "since it's a nasty bird that fouls its own nest." Tone also explained Sasso's teaching responsibilities for the fall semester. Tone would place all student teachers and would handle any problems that arose in the schools. Sasso was to limit his role to observing the students and to reporting any problems to Tone. When Sasso protested that such an arrangement would make it impossible for him to establish rapport with the student teachers and to work effectively with the supervising teachers, Tone replied that *he* already had an "excellent working relationship with students and teachers" and that was all that was necessary.

On the day before classes began, Tone directed all department members to report to his office to assist with student registration. When Sasso arrived, he found his three colleagues sitting quietly on a bench outside Tone's office. Students filed one at a time into Tone's office to be registered. Tone worked out their schedule and approved their course selections. It was clear to the students from day one where all authority and control resided and where all questions concerning programs, policies, and problems were to be deferred. Sasso

123

watched the proceedings for half an hour before leaving to work at the resource center. That afternoon Sasso received a strongly-worded note from Tone directing him to "remain at his post" on all future assignments unless "told to do otherwise by the chairperson."

During the first week of classes, Sasso accompanied Tone on the trips to place student teachers in the schools. Eight students at a time were loaded in the van and driven around to the various schools where teachers were asked to supervise them. Tone had made no preliminary contacts with the schools, and principals and teachers were frequently annoyed by the sudden appearance of several Meridith students outside their office or classroom doors while school was in session. Tone would move from room to room seeking to persuade teachers to take a student teacher, and as he begged, flattered, wheedled, and cajoled, embarassed Meridith students paced nervously nearby. Some teachers would refuse outright while others, after excessive pleading by Tone, would carefully look over the group before selecting a student teacher. Sasso did not join the negotiations but rather chose to remain with the students, talking to them quietly and seeking to reassure them. After several students had been placed, Tone suddenly ordered Sasso to join him in trying to persuade teachers to accept students. Sasso suggested that current procedures stop, and that placement be arranged prior to classes, without the students being present, and with teachers who had expressed an interest in supervising student teachers. A bitter exchange followed in the presence of the students with Tone accusing Sasso of insubordination and with Sasso denouncing Tone's procedures as poorly planned, ineffective, and "demeaning" to the students who were being treated as if they were "a litter of puppies awaiting selection."

Word of the Tone-Sasso exchange spread rapidly among the graduate students who began to view Sasso as their champion and as a buffer against Tone' authoritarian rule. Sasso sought to avoid confrontation with Tone, but there appeared to be little he could do that did not result in Tone's displeasure. Sasso worked well with the principals, supervising teachers, and student teachers at the schools where he observed. He was knowledgeable, articulate, patient, and because of his classroom teaching experience, he could readily identify with his student teachers' needs and problems. He was particularly popular with the staff at Summit Street School—a dilapidated building in the inner city with a student body of disadvantages children. When he expressed an interest in having his methods course students work with the disadvantaged, he was invited to establish a program engaging them as teacher aides in the school. Sasso submitted his program plans to the Research Coordinator at Meridith and received the Coordinator's approval along with a small grant from the university's research promotion fund to pay for student transportation and for materials for enrichment projects students would develop. The program proved to be an immediate success with student aides averaging six hours of class time per week on enrichment lessons ranging from creative writing to art projects. It also provided Sasso with excellent research material, and he wrote two major articles which were published in professional journals. However, regardless of this program's success, Tone's criticisms of Sasso continued. In a curt note to Sasso, he complained that the program should have first been approved by him and then it should have been presented as a "departmental project" with the department receiving full credit for it.

As the semester progressed Tone recognized that Sasso was becoming increasingly popular with the students, and he felt that much of this popularity was attained at his expense. He sought to mask his differences with Sasso and even befriended him before the students on several occasions. But shortly after mid-semester an incident occurred that ended any pretense of a harmonious working relationship between the two men. It also drove many of the graduate students to express open support for Sasso against Tone.

Tone's method of placing student teachers ruled out any possibility of matching supervisor with student teacher nor did it allow for the matching of specific schools with the special needs, interests, personality, training, and skills of the student teacher. Consequently, each semester several students were badly misplaced, and the student teaching experience proved disappointing, disillusioning, and depressing. These students had no recourse; Tone would not reassign them even if the principal and supervising teacher supported such a request. With Sasso visiting the schools, all of this changed. Working closely with all involved, but not informing Tone of his actions, Sasso reassigned a male and two female student teachers who were having difficulties. Shortly after these changes were made, Sasso became ill with the flu and Tone visited the schools in his place. When Tone discovered that Sasso had made changes without his consent, he became enraged. He interrupted lessons in each of the classes taught by the reassigned student teachers and demanded to know why they were not teaching in their "assigned classes." In the exchanges that followed, the two female student teachers burst into tear and wept helplessly before the students, the male teacher made an obscene gesture to

Tone and attempted to continue teaching his lesson. In each class, the supervising teacher had to take over the class to restore order, and Tone was asked to leave the room.

The following day Tone met with Sasso and gave him a two-part directive in writing. First, Sasso was to stop visiting the schools where the teaching reassignments had been made; Tone would observe and grade the reassigned students. Second, Sasso was to confine all visits at other schools to observing student teachers; he was to report any problems arising in the schools to Tone and "under no circumstances attempt to handle them in any way". Tone also warned Sasso that he would periodically check all the schools Sasso visited. Sasso attempted to explain why the reassignments were necessary, but Tone refused to listen and suggested that Sasso had become a "loose cannon" in the education department.

Tone's treatment of Sasso and of the reassigned student teachers led many graduate students in the education department to write letters of protest to the dean of the graduate school and to the president of the university. For the first time in his career, Tone was confronted by hostile students who openly challenged his actions. However, the graduate school dean, who was an old and close friend of Tone, hesitated to act on the letters, and the president, Earl Smithson, made no public comment on them.

During this difficult period, Sasso applied for a position at Alton College, a small public teachers' college, located in his native state. The position was tailor-made for someone with Sasso's credentials and experience. It was for a specialist in methods and student teacher supervision who could also offer courses in the foundations or philosophy of education area. The position was at the assistant professor rank. It required five years in rank as a condition for consideration for promotion or tenure, and it paid ten percent less than Sasso's current salary. Alton was an undergraduate school that accepted any student who graduated from a public high school in the state. All faculty taught five courses per semester and class sizes were large. The emphasis was upon teaching and service; there was little concern about research and publication. When Sasso visited the campus for a job interview, he found the education department faculty to be friendly and the chairperson to be personable, objective, and receptive to the ideas of others. Sasso impressed the department favorably, and before he left campus he was offered the job and given a January 20th deadline for his decision.

Sasso told no one at the university about his job offer. In the weeks remaining before the end of the semester, he sought to distance himself from Tone and to avoid confrontation; but the conflicts continued. At a doctoral candidate's oral examination, Tone belittled Sasso's comments and the acrimonious exchange that followed ended only after committee members intervened. When Tone rejected Sasso's request to continue the Summit Street School teacher-aide program for the second semester, Sasso denounced Tone for being "stupid, callous, and arbitrary." Sasso appealed Tone's decision to the Research Coordinator who overruled Tone and provided funding for the program to continue. Finally, a bitter confrontation occurred when supervising teachers warned Sasso that Tone had been visiting them, suggesting that Sasso was incompetent, and encouraging them to file complaints against him.

On the last day of classes Sasso received the following letter from Tone.

**Dear Dr. Sasso:**

Before the end of this first semestar it has seem that an assessment of your work was in order. In light of your reactions to some earlier verbal reports and reactions tl you during the semester, it appears to be wisest to put the following in written form.

I am sorry, as Department Chairman, to have to tell to you that, in spite of some real assests which you have, our over-all appraisal of your work has not been that it has been satisfactory, particularly in your inter-personal relations with members of the Staff in the Department anl in som of xxxxx of your contracts with Supervising Teachers and Principals of scholes in which our student teaching was being conducted.

You seem to have a personaliti problem and will not except necessary rules and regulations made by those in authority who know better. From the point of view the important ingrediant for successgul schllarly work and the successfil operation of My Department is obediance from all members of the staff. In may opinion this ingrediant has been particularly absent in relation to your work and attitude with us since at least mid-semester.

From the point of view of your professional development and for what is best for My department, I would advise you to seek a position elsewhere. I would also sugest you seek psychiatric counseling..

Very Truly Yours,
Harlan Tone
Chairman, Education Department

Sasso discussed the letter with his wife. Deidre was emotionally drained from all the fighting. She questioned Tone's "mental stability" and urged her husband to take the Alton position. She was anxious for the family to return home to where it was "peaceful and quiet." Sasso agreed that the constant conflict was exhausting. He felt that the contents of the letter and the way it was written confirmed the serious doubts he also held about Tone's emotional state. The next day he submitted a letter of resignation to President Smithson informing him that he was accepting a position at Alton College and would be leaving Meridith at the end of the second semester.

President Smithson wrote to Sasso requesting a meeting and counseling him not to act "precipitously." At the meeting Sasso recounted the chain of events that led to his resignation and showed Smithson the letter from Tone. Smithson was visibly shaken by the letter and asked Sasso not to resign. He explained the deal made with Tone when Tone left the psychology department, and he expressed the fear that if he "reneged on this deal in anyway" he would polarize the faculty by alienating many of the older and more distinguished members who felt sorry for Tone. He admitted that he had received numerous letters from students, supervising teachers, and principals complaining that Tone's administrative policies and procedures were "authoritarian, arbitrary, callous, and capricious." In contrast he had heard "nothing but praise" for Sasso's teaching and for the field work he had been doing with the students and the schools.

Smithson then offered Sasso a deal. Since he could not afford to polarize his faculty by forcing Tone to step down as chairperson, he would allow Tone to remain at this post for one more year at which time Tone would turn 65, the mandatory retirement age for all administrative positions. Smithson would then appoint Sasso acting department head and would strongly recommend he be appointed chairperson on a permanent basis. Sasso would also receive an increase in salary equivalent to twenty percent more than he would receive at Alton College, and at the end of the year, Smithson would recommend him for tenure and promotion to associate professor. As part of the deal, Sasso would develop a "blind eye" and a "deaf ear" to Tone's eccentricities and to his "enlightened despot" approach to administrative policies and procedures. Sasso would avoid all confrontation and would encourage students to cooperate with Tone and abide by his directives.

Tone was never to learn of this deal. Smithson would meet with Tone and Sasso to heal the existent rift and to encourage them to work together. He would support Tone's role as chairperson, and he would praise Sasso's fieldwork with the students and his publications and research resulting from his program with the disadvantaged. Sasso would "express regrets" over incidents that had occurred during the past semester, and he would affirm his "desire to cooperate and work closely with Tone in the future."

Smithson asked Sasso to reconsider his resignation and to accept the deal. He pointed out to Sasso that the position at Meridith, unlike that at Alton, allowed him to work with small classes bright, highly-motivated graduate students, and it allowed him to remain on the "cutting edge of knowledge" by requiring him to engage in scholarly research and publication. He also reminded Sasso that the graduate students in the education department needed him; they had openly sided with him against Tone and would be left in an "extremely vulnerable position" if Sasso left. He gave Sasso until January 20th to decide.

On the evening of January 18th, Sasso sat at his desk and prepared to compose letters to Meridith University and to Alton College. He had a difficult decision to make. Should he remain at Meridith and continue to work under Tone for another year or should he accept the position at Alton and leave Meridith? What should he do?

# Study Guide for Case #13

To the Instructor and Student:

This guide is designed to assist the student in analyzing this case in the following ways. It suggests:

1. a major *Area of Educational Concern* that is central to the case and upon which the student should focus his/her research efforts.

2. *Concepts* that are related to key dimensions of the case and that the student should seek to understand. These *Concepts* have broad implications for educational theory and practice and are listed as *Pivotal Terms*.

3. *Questions* that are concerned with problems raised by the case and that the student should explore further for possible issues;

4. *Reference Material* that is related to the case and that the student should use as a resource in researching the case;

## Case #13
### *"The Deal"*

1. *Area of Educational Concern:* How should policy be formulated and change implemented in an educational institution?

2. *Concepts-Pivotal Terms:*

| | |
|---|---|
| "Peter principle" | student teacher |
| disadvantaged | supervising teacher |
| inner city schools | tenure |
| burnout | differential staffing |
| curriculum resource center | philosophy of education |
| job satisfaction | need fulfillment |
| research/publish | faculty morale |
| role model | post-doctoral studies |
| refereed professional journal | student evaluation |
| American Assoc. of | |
|     University Professors | pedantic |
| classroom observation | authoritarian |

3. *Questions:*

Should administrators rely upon "making deals" in the course of developing policy and implementing change?

How important is self-expression on the job?

Do educational institutions have responsibilities/obligations to faculty members who, with age, lose their effectiveness as scholars and/or teachers?

How much input should students have in the evaluation of faculty?

What should be the relationship between the universities/colleges and the elementary/secondary schools regarding the placement, supervision, and evaluation of student teachers?

What should be the responsibilities of a department chairperson?

What should the role of a professor focus upon—teaching or research and publication?

Are authoritarian administrative practices self-defeating?

4. *Reference Material:*

Blank, Mary A. and Heathington, Betty S. (1987). The supervisory process: A consistent approach to help student teachers improve. *The Teacher Educator,* 22(4), 2–14.

Dewey, Jack. (1986). *Burned Out!* Shelburne, VT: The New England Press.

Fuchs, Gordon E. and Louise P. Moore. (1988). Collaberation for understanding and effectiveness. *The Clearing House,* 5(1), 410–413.

Joyce, Bernard and Showers, Beverly. (1982). The coaching of teaching. *Education Leadership,* 40(1), 4–10.

Loken, Gregory. (1988). Staking a claim. *Social Policy,* 19(1), 13–16.

Marshall, James. (1985). *The Devil in the Classroom.* New York: Schocken.

Ravitch, Diane. (1983). Scapegoating the teachers. *The New Republic,* 189(19), 27–29.

Reuben, Brent D. (1984). *Communication and Human Behavior.*
New York: Macmillan.

# A Question of Religious Beliefs

During the twenty-five years following the Korean War, the suburban community of Sunton underwent dramatic changes. A mass influx of middle class residents from two large neighboring cities had swelled its population from 40,000 to 150,000 and had transformed its sparsely settled, semi-rural environment into a heavily developed, residential area. This population explosion sharply altered the religious makeup of Sunton as well. From a Protestant community that had few Catholics and no Jewish residents, it became a Jewish community with less than forty percent of its residents Christian.

The Sunton School System expanded to meet the needs of the growing student population. Twelve elementary school, four middle schools, and two high schools were built. These new schools were headed by personnel promoted chiefly from the teaching staffs of the system's older schools; consequently, more than ninety percent of Sunton's school administrators were Christians. Similarly, Sunton's teaching staff was mostly Christian since these administrators chose to do most of their recruiting at a neighboring small, private college of Christian denomination.

The student body in the new schools reflected the religious shift in Sunton's population. In all of them, less than twenty percent of the children were Christian. These schools did not observe traditional Christmas activities, and only infrequent references were made to Chanukha and Christmas or holiday trees. Parents of the Christian minority, who were unhappy with this failure to observe Christmas in the schools, complained to the Superintendent, Dr. Marjorie Swift, but

133

she had tended to play down their comments while allowing the schools to continue in their policy.

In Sunton's older schools, the Christian children remained in the majority, but the Jewish minority grew to almost forty percent of the student body. These schools continued to allow the traditional Christmas activities which included singing Christmas carols, holding dramatic presentations of the birth of Jesus, and displaying art projects and bulletin boards focusing upon the Nativity. Parents of the Jewish minority, who were unhappy with these Christian religious observances during school time, complained to the Superintendent, but she also minimized their comments and allowed the schools to continue the activities.

The Superintendent, who assumed office several years earlier, found that her strategy of avoiding open support of either religious group while allowing majority rule at each school to determine the continuation of Christmas activities, had met with considerable success. There were no major confrontations between the groups over Christmas activities, and there appeared to be an harmonious relationship among the children of different religions in the schools. All of this changed in the fall of 1985 when Sam Howe was promoted Chairman of the Guidance Department at Grey Latin Middle School which was the oldest school in the Sunton System.

Sam Howe was one of the first Jewish teachers in the Sunton System. He had been hired during the acute teacher shortage of the late 1960's, and he had been a counselor in the first new middle school built to accommodate the growing student population. Sam quickly established himself as a conscientious and concerned counselor, and he became very popular with the students and parents. His quick mind and natural leadership qualities also earned him the friendship and respect of the faculty and administration. He was anxious to remain well-informed and to become an authority in his field, and by 1978, he had earned a Master's Degree and a Certificate of Advanced Graduate Study in the areas of counseling and administration. When the chairman's position became vacant at Grey Latin Middle School, Sam was easily the most qualified applicant and was appointed to it.

The Grey Latin Middle School was an attractive structure of Renaissance style located in the oldest and wealthiest neighborhood in Sunton. It seemed to belong among the tree-lined streets and stately Georgian and Victorian mansions that housed the political, social, and economic leaders of Sunton. Grey Latin was noted for its excellent traditional course offerings and for its cultural-enrichment program of drama, art, and music. Most of its graduates went on to Smith Classical High School and, ultimately, on to the more prestigious higher institutions of learning in the area.

Sam Howe was familiar with Grey Latin's fine reputation, and he had enrolled two of his children in the school. He welcomed the opportunity to become part of a faculty which he believed played a critical role in the shaping of future professional leaders of the community. Sam's initial contacts with the students and parents proved to be very fruitful. During the first three months of the fall term, he became known among his advisees as a patient, understanding, and informed friend who always had their well-being in mind when he offered constructive criticisms and advice. He also addressed the local Parent Teachers Association, became active in its programs, and quickly established a reputation among parents as an educator concerned with their children's welfare.

Both of Sam's children had sought to take advantage of the fine arts program at Grey Latin. Sam's older boy, Joel, was in the eighth grade drama class while his younger daughter, Deborah, was in the girls' chorus and participated in the seventh grade music program. Late in November, the faculty at Grey Latin began to organize their classes around the upcoming scheduled Christmas activities. The drama class prepared a play on the Nativity to be presented to the parents and students on the final day of school before the holiday vacation. Joel Howe was selected for the role of one of the Magi. The girls' chorus was organized into groups of carolers who would visit several of the elementary schools and present music programs focusing upon the birth of Christ. Deborah Howe was selected to lead one of the groups.

Deborah and Joel discussed with their father their ambivalence toward participating in the Christmas activities. On the one hand, they had found the fine arts program to be particularly rewarding, and they enjoyed considerable success and popularity with their teachers and classmates. Consequently, they wanted to remain in the program and share its activities with their classmates. On the other hand, they firmly believed in Judaism, understood its tenets, and were devoted observers of the Judaic holidays. According to their religious beliefs, they viewed Jesus as an interesting character, a great teacher and charismatic leader, but they did not believe he was a prophet and Messiah. Consequently, they held a negative view of the religious significance of Jesus and felt trapped in the hypocrisy of being forced to participate in Christmas activities that glorified Jesus as the Christ.

Sam met with Joseph Coutier, who taught the drama class, and Mary Sweet, who headed the girls' chorus, and informed them of his children's feelings. He told them he had directed his children to absent themselves from the fine arts program and to attend study hall until after the Christmas activities had been performed. He also expressed his personal dismay at the school's insensitivity to its Jewish pupils who made up thirty-five percent of the student body. He found it inconceivable that Jewish students be required to either participate in or to observe Christmas activities which so patently ignored their religious convictions.

Both teachers expressed sharp disagreement with Sam's statements and action. They felt Christmas was an integral part of the American cultural experience and should be observed by the schools. Further, they interpreted Joel and Deborah's refusal to attend classes as an act of official withdrawal, and they dropped them from the fine arts program for the remainder of the school year.

The news of Sam's rebelling against the Christmas activities spread quickly throughout Grey Latin and triggered a major religious controversy that spilled beyond the confines of the school. Within one week after Joel and Deborah stopped participating in the fine arts program large numbers of Jewish children followed suit, and the drama class lost nine of its best students while the girls' chorus lost one-fourth of its members. Two of the local rabbis issued strong public endorsements of the action of parents who withdrew the children from the program. They also wrote to Superintendent Swift requesting that Grey Latin discontinue all Christmas activities. The local chapter of the American Civil Liberties Union also wrote to Superintendent Swift and warned that the school could be subject to legal action for violation of the First Amendment's requirement of separation of church and state. A majority of the faculty at Grey Latin responded with a petition to the superintendent stating that the activities should be continued because Christmas was a vital part of the national heritage. Several local ministers followed with strong letters in support of observing Christmas in the schools. A group of lawyers, whose children had attended Gray Latin, placed an advertisement in the local newspaper citing a number of court cases which they felt supported the continuation of Christmas observances in public schools. Sunton's major newspaper also carried an editorial on the controversy along with numerous letters to the editor supporting and attacking the continuation of Christmas activities.

As each day passed, the number of letters and phone calls to the superintendent's office from parents grew, and their tone became increasingly strident, emotional, and bigoted. Superintendent Swift could no longer avoid confronting the issue. She must make a decision either to allow Christmas activities or to discontinue them altogether. What should she do?

# Study Guide for Case #14

To the Instructor and Student::

This guide is designed to assist the student in analyzing this case in the following ways. It suggests:

1.  a major *Area of Educational Concern* that is central to the case and upon which the student should focus his/her research efforts.

2.  *Concepts* that are related to key dimensions of the case and that the student should seek to understand. These *Concepts* have broad implications for educational theory and practice and are listed as *Pivotal Terms*.

3.  *Questions* that are concerned with problems raised by the case and that the student should explore further for possible issues;

4.  *Reference Material* that is related to the case and that the student should use as a resource in researching the case;

## Case #14

*"A Question of Beliefs"*

1.  *Area of Educational Concern:* What should be the role of religion in our schools?

2.  *Concepts-Pivotal Terms:*

| | |
|---|---|
| social mobility | religious pluralism |
| First Amendment | alienation |
| captive audience | Florey v. Sioux Falls |
| enculturation | local control |
| Fourteenth Amendment | parental consent |
| secularism | normative vs. descriptive |
| Establishment Clause | cultural heritage |
| Free Exercise Clause | fine arts program |
| Certif. of Advanced Grad. Study | ACLU |
| bigot | shared/released time |
| pluralistic pageants | socialization |

3. *Questions:*

   To what extent should a school program/curriculum reflect the norms, mores, values, and attitudes of the local community it serves?

   Can schools remain free of sectarian indoctrination while allowing observances of Christmas, or any other religious activities, in their classroom?

   Should schools require all children to learn about the religions of the world?

   How do you determine secular areas of schooling from non-secular?

   Why has the question of religion in the schools remained a major issue of concern to most Americans?

   Should children attend school where their parents teach?

   How can schools in our pluralistic society adapt to religious diversity?

   Does moral or religious instruction have a role in public education?

4. *Reference Material:*

   Beck, Clive. (1985). Religion and education. *Teachers College Record,* 87(2), 259–276.

   Bole, William. (1987). Celebrating Christmas in public schools. *Christ Today,* 31(8), 55–56.

   Collie, William. (1983). Schempp reconsidered: The relationship between religion and public education. *Phi Delta Kappan,* 65(1), 57–59.

   Crewdson, Robert L. (1987). The Equal Access Act of 1984. *Journal of Law and Education,* 16(2), 168–172.

   McCarthy, Martha M. (1985). Religion and public schools: Emerging legal standards and unresolved issues. *Harvard Educational Review,* 55(3), 278–317.

   Schimmel, David. (1988). Constitutional imperatives for the public schools. *The High School Journal,* 71(4), 200–205.

Sendor, Benjamin. (1985). How to distinguish religion from curriculum. *American School Board Journal*, 172(7), 18; 44.

Zakariya, Sally Banks. (1984). Celebrate the holiday season by teaching kids about their world. *American School Board Journal*, 171(2), 41–41.

# The Choice

When old Mr. Peterson retired as Spanish teacher at Lafayette High in Pleasantville, it was a foregone conclusion among the faculty that Randy Scott would be his replacement. It almost seemed as if Randy had been preparing for the Peterson position all his life, and now that it was vacant students, parents, and faculty felt he should fill it.

Randy had Mr. Peterson twenty-seven years ago when he was a student at Lafayette. Spanish had always been his favorite subject, and if financial circumstances had permitted, Randy would have gone to State Teachers College and trained to become a Spanish teacher. But his father had deserted his mother, and Randy, as the oldest of three children, had to work while he was in high school to help support the family. At graduation, Randy joined the army and for the next twenty-five years made the armed services his career. He proved to be an effective soldier and natural leader, and he rose quickly in the ranks. He became an officer, distinguished himself in the Korean and Vietnam Wars, and was stationed in Europe for a six-year tour-of-duty in Spain. While in Spain, his facility with languages led to his appointment as chief liaison officer responsible for maintaining harmony and promoting cooperation with the officials of towns surrounding a large American military base.

During his years in the service, Randy completed the equivalent of three years of college work through USAFI courses and attended various college programs sponsored by the military. When Randy retired from the army, he resettled in Pleasantville with his wife and two children. He completed his senior year at State Teachers College and did his student teaching at Lafayette High under Mr. Peterson. There were no teaching jobs when he graduated, but Randy chose to retain his ties with Lafayette and became a substitute teacher on daily call for less than $50.00 per day. He was frequently asked to replace Mr. Peterson who had become quite ill as he approached retirement.

Randy proved to be effective and popular both as a student teacher and a substitute teacher. He enjoyed working with children, loved his subject matter, and communicated an infectious enthusiasm to all his classes. He did not agree with Mr. Peterson's traditional approach to teaching Spanish, and he was anxious to experiment in a more progressive vein with the hope of making the language relevant to the students' daily lives by focusing upon its cultural context. When Mr. Peterson submitted his resignation, Randy applied for the position and received strong support in letters of recommendation from Mr. Peterson and several members of the faculty and community.

Over the years Lafayette High had enjoyed considerable federal assistance without it ever having its policies as an equal opportunity employer questioned. It had received several large federal grants for specialized courses in reading, math, and science, and it had applied for additional funding for an experimental program in foreign language instruction. But federal funding had become increasingly difficult to obtain as Lafayette's hiring policies had become suspect and an object of criticism. Eighty percent of its faculty were male, and over the last ten years, five vacant positions were all filled by males. Further, while eleven percent of the students body was black, it had never employed a black faculty member and had never actively sought to recruit one. Thus, when Superintendent Bill Comte received Mr. Peterson's resignation, he seized upon this vacancy as the perfect vehicle for dispelling any suggestions of racist/sexist hiring policies and for regaining a favorable rating as an equal opportunity employer. With considerable fanfare, using all of the avenues of the media available to him, Comte advertised the position widely and encouraged all qualified candidates to apply regardless of race, color, religion or sex.

This posted position fell upon a job market that was saturated with unemployed teachers, and Superintendent Comte's office was inundated with over three-hundred applications from several states in the region. To screen the candidates, he appointed a committee consisting of the principal of Lafayette, the chairman of the language department, two teachers, and two members of the Parent Teacher Association. The committee was to submit the names of two candidates, and he would select one of them for the position. After weeks of deliberation, which included interviewing the most promising applicants, the committee recommended Randy Scott and Felicia Brown, The committee accompanied its recommendations with a statement of its observations of the applicants' strengths and weaknesses and the rationale for its selections.

Randy Scott was selected because of his broad background and considerable practical experience with the Spanish language and culture while he was in the service. It was felt he could make the subject matter challenging and exciting, placing it within a cultural context in which it would "come alive" and secure the students' interests. Among his assets were the following. He was mature, well-rounded and had held responsible leadership positions as he served his country well in war and in peace. He had taught in the school system, was familiar with the operations of the school, and was respected and accepted by faculty, students, and parents. He had enjoyed a rich, cultural experience in Spain where he utilized his language skills in daily interactions with the local people from all walks of life. Finally, it was felt that he had proven his loyalty and commitment to the school system by serving as a substitute teacher for little pay. Among his liabilities were the following. At age forty-six, his teaching career would be of relatively short duration—less than twenty years. He had only average grades on his college transcript, receiving mostly Bs and Cs in USAFI correspondence courses. He had a relatively limited academic preparation enabling him to meet only the very minimal state certification requirements in language and education courses. This could limit both his understanding of, and teaching approach to, the complexities of syntax and other dimensions of grammar in the Spanish language.

Felicia Brown was selected because of her extensive training and preparation and her fine academic record. It was felt she could make the subject matter challenging and exciting, utilizing a rich variety of teaching strategies and methodologies that would invite student involvement, appeal to specific interests, and satisfy individual needs. She had been the first black student in the area to be awarded a National Merit Scholarship to an ivy league school where she graduated Phi Beta Kappa with a Bachelor of Arts degree in Spanish. She had also completed a Master of Arts in Teaching degree and had received extensive training in specialized courses in the teaching of languages.

In recommending her, the committee felt she was the type of qualified candidate an equal opportunity employer should seriously consider if race and sex were not to be barriers to employment.

Among her assets were the following. She had received extensive preparation in the Spanish language, having taken twice the number of courses required for state certification. She had a in-depth training in the most recent methods and materials involved in teaching foreign languages. She had been given high recommendations from her professors and supervising teacher. She had achieved an excellent academic record at one of the most prestigious universities in the country. Finally, it was felt that she would provide an excellent role model for the black students at the school. Among her liabilities were the following. She had limited experience in actual classroom teaching, and other than her student teaching, she had never worked in any capacity with teenagers. She had never traveled abroad and, therefore, lacked immediate exposure to the Spanish language, people, and culture. Finally, she had no previous contact with the Lafayette school and was totally unfamiliar with its operations, it faculty, and its students.

The selection committee had done its job well, and Superintendent Comte was confronted with a difficult choice. What should he do? Should he hire Randy Scott or Felicia Brown?

# Study Guide for Case #15

To the Instructor and Student:

This guide is designed to assist the student in analyzing this case in the following ways. It suggests:

1. a major *Area of Educational Concern* that is central to the case and upon which the student should focus his/her research efforts.

2. *Concepts* that are related to key dimensions of the case and that the student should seek to understand. These *Concepts* have broad implications for educational theory and practice and are listed as *Pivotal Terms*.

3. *Questions* that are concerned with problems raised by the case and that the student should explore further for possible issues;

4. *Reference Material* that is related to the case and that the student should use as a resource in researching the case;

## Case #15

*"The Choice"*

1. *Area of Educational Concern:* What qualifications should we seek in teacher candidates that will best predict their competency and effectiveness in the classroom?

2. *Concepts-Pivotal Terms:*

| | |
|---|---|
| equal opportunity employer | essentialism: reason |
| certification requirements | reverse discrimination |
| teacher preparation courses | teacher competency |
| progressivism: experience | USAFI |
| role model | substitute teacher |
| traditional:structured | single-parent family |
| federal aid | minority |
| sexist hiring policy | Parent Teacher Association |
| cultural context | transcript |
| teaching methodologies | National Merit Scholarship |
| Phi Beta Kappa | racist hiring policy |

3. *Questions:*

Should such factors as being an equal opportunity employer and/or having veteran status play a role in the selection and hiring of teachers?

What is the most effective way to prepare future language teachers for the classroom?

What input should lay persons in the community have in the selection and hiring of teachers?

Should language teachers be required to travel and study in foreign countries?

How important are courses in instructional methods for language teachers?

What personality qualities, background experiences, and educational preparation and training, should be considered in projecting the success of a teacher candidate?

Is the equal opportunity law necessary?

4. *Reference Material:*

Bennie, William A. (1982). Field-based teacher education—A reconsideration? *The Teacher Educator,* 17(4), 19–24.

Brackamp, Larry. (1984). *Evaluating Teacher Effectiveness.* Beverly Hills, CA: Sage.

Bundy, McGeorge. (1978). Beyond Bakke, what future affirmative action? *The Atlantic,* 242(5), 69–73.

Cruckshank, Donald R. (1986). Profile of an effective teacher. *Educational Horizons,* 64(2), 80–86.

Darling, Linda. (1986). Teacher evaluation: A proposal. *Education Digest,* 52(11), 30–33.

Duke, Daniel L. and Richard J. Stiggins. (1986). *Teacher Evaluation.* Washington, DC: National Education Association.

Goldhammer, Keith. (1982). Hallmarks for excellence in teacher education. *Education Digest,* 47(7), 39–41.

Perry, Nancy C. (1981). New Teachers: Do the best get hired? *Phi Delta Kappan,* 63(2), 113–114.

# Abbeville's Dilemma

Since the turn of the twentieth century, when State College was first located within the outskirts of Abbeville, an uneasy truce had existed between the staff and students of the land-grant college and the residents of the town. Abbeville was a rural community located near the ocean, and its chief income was from fishing, farming, and tourism. The outlook of its residents was narrow, limited, and unsophisticated. They viewed the college community as "outsiders," and they sought to keep the control of the town in the hands of "natives." Consequently, during the first fifty years of the College's existence, it had very little social and political intercourse with the town. Faculty members were rarely elected to town offices, and college students were welcomed only by the small shopkeepers and merchants who profited from their patronage.

The residents of Abbeville enjoyed a low tax rate, and they opposed any municipal projects that would raise taxes. During the 1930's when the Works Progress Administration was erecting buildings at no cost to the towns, they allowed it to build their elementary, middle, and high schools, but they rejected a sewer project, and a police station when they were asked to pay ten percent of the cost. They also retained a volunteer fire department, rejected a reservoir project, and refused to contribute to the construction of a spur track that was essential to the several industries struggling to locate in the area.

In the years following W. W. II the population of Abbeville underwent a gradual but dramatic change. Veterans taking advantage of the GI Bill enrolled in large numbers at State College. They were followed in the 1950s and 1960s by other students throughout the state who were unable to afford the rising tuition rates of private colleges. By the late 1970s State College, with over 10,000 students, had quadrupled in size, and it boasted a large resident faculty and graduate student body. This population expansion at the College was paralleled by a similar growth of two other groups. Large numbers of retirees, seeking to escape the blight of the large cities in the state, had found a haven of beauty and tranquility in the countrified environment of Abbeville. They were able to purchase relatively inexpensive homes and enjoy a very low tax rate. Similarly, large numbers of the professional and managerial class, fleeing from urban blight and suburban sprawl, found in the peaceful, rural setting of Abbeville an ideal location to build their palatial homes and acquire sizable land holdings.

By the mid-1960s the population expansion had placed such severe strains upon Abbeville's limited and primitive municipal facilities that some desperately needed improvements had to be made. Over a five year period property was reevaluated and tax rates were increased in order to build a police station, establish a full-time fire department, set aside land for a reservoir, and provide wage increases for teachers.

By the late 1960s the tax rate had risen over three hundred percent and a group of taxpayers revolted and formed the Citizen's Association to Curtail Tax Increases. It consisted of sixty percent of Abbeville's registered voters with a membership chiefly of farmers, fishermen, and retirees. The Association carefully monitored all financial town meetings and organized large voter turnouts to defeat any proposals that would increase taxes. Opposed to this Association was a small but extremely articulate group made up of members from the college community and of homeowners from the professional and managerial classes.

In the late 1970s the shortcomings of Abbeville's municipal facilities generated a dual crisis, and the taxpayers became locked in a struggle to determine how best to resolve it. The marine biology department of State College, operating under a federal grant, undertook a study of the conditions of Abbeville's rivers and waterways. The study found traces of pollutants in the waters that could present a potential health hazard in future years if they continued to increase in quantity and were not removed. It was noted that the sources of these pollutants, which included the hospital, various public buildings in town, and many older homes, were dumping raw sewerage into the waters in ever increasing amounts. Further, it was discovered that many of the cesspools and leaching fields of newly-built homes were inadequate, and sewerage runoffs in fields and open areas were common.

The study prompted state health officials and the Environmental Protection Agency to issue warnings to Abbeville and to recommend the installation of a sewerage system and treatment plant. The town council applied for federal aid and was promised funds to subsidize sixty percent of the cost of construction if the system was completed within three years. An engineering firm estimated that the town costs would be five million dollars and that each resident connecting into the system would be charged an additional fourteen hundred dollars. The town tax assessor estimated the tax rate would have to be raised ninety percent over the next five years to meet the debts incurred by installation of the system.

While the residents of Abbeville were wrestling with the sewerage problem, a second and equally costly crisis emerged in the schools. The children of families who had settled in the town during the postwar years had begun to attend the high school in large numbers, and serious overcrowding had resulted. The high school had classroom space for 800 students, and enrollments had reached 1,000 and were expected to increase to over 1400 within five years. The school's facilities, especially its laboratories, library, cafeteria, and gymnasiums were inadequate to meet the needs of this growing student population. The superintendent of schools warned the town council that the quality of education was being seriously undermined and that unless this situation was relieved in the immediate future, the school would lose it regional accreditation, and its students would have difficulty gaining admission to higher institutions of learning.

The council responded to the superintendent's warning by having the state department of education study the problem and make recommendations. The state department's study suggested that a new high school containing all of the latest educational technology and facilities be built at a cost of three and one-half million dollars. It noted that during the year in which the school was being built, the existing school could avoid loss of accreditation by adopting a double session program. The study expressed reservations concerning any extended use of double session which it viewed as an "emergency measure that would prove counterproductive over time." It warned of the following inherent disadvantages of double session. Competitive athletics, intramural sports, band, and other extracurricular activities of a social and educational value that were usually scheduled during after school hours would be eliminated or curtailed. After school sessions scheduled for disciplining students and for providing remedial work for students in academic difficulty would also be curtailed. Maintenance costs for the school building would increase dramatically as limited facilities subjected to continuous overuse would deteriorate and break down. The safety of school children would be jeopardized during the winter months as they waited to take school buses in the dark hours before dawn and at dusk. The study concluded with this warning.

"Double session will end overcrowding and will remove the threat of loss of accreditation. But this could only prove to be a temporary reprieve. If the student population continues to increase, as demographic trends indicate, the building of a new school could become even more imperative. For within five years, *both* sessions of the old school could become overcrowded and loss of accreditation would follow."

The state department study was followed by a report from the town tax assessor which estimated the tax rate would have to be raised seventy-five percent over the next five years to meet the debt incurred in building the school. The report also reminded the council of a study made a year earlier by the community planning department of State College which had warned that while some residents of Abbeville could easily afford an increase of more than 100 percent in the tax rate over the next five years, others on a fixed incomes (retirees) and with a small family business (farmers and fishermen) would suffer considerable financial hardship from such a tax raise and could find it impossible to absorb. The assessor concluded with a strong recommendation that the council select one of the projects for immediate construction and delay the other for at least five years.

The town council voted unanimously to accept the assessor's recommendation to construct either the sewerage system or the school, but its five members were badly divided as to which project should be built first. Two members favored the sewerage project and two wanted the new school The deciding vote would have to be cast by the council president, Amos Parker.

Amos Parker was a native of Abbeville. His ancestors were among the town's founders, and for more than two-hundred years the Parker farm had shipped produce throughout the state. Amos had earned an engineering degree from State College and for the past twenty years had commuted more than sixty miles to a neighboring city where he headed a small construction firm. Amos was extremely popular with the residents of Abbeville and had been elected to the council for an unprecedented five terms. He took considerable pride in the town, and was a leading advocate for cleaner water and for improved education.

Amos recognized that if the pollution of Abbeville's waters continued unabated, a potential health hazard would be allowed to develop unchecked, and the problems of restoring these waters to the former cleanliness would become greatly magnified. He also recognized that if overcrowding continued in the old high school and double session was adopted for an extended period of time, the quality of education would suffer and accreditation would be lost. Further, he realized that his four children, would shortly be attending the high school, and he would prefer they benefit from the latest educational technology and facilities that a new school would provide.

The other four members of the council are waiting for Amos to cast his vote. What should he do? Should he vote to build the sewerage system immediately and delay the new school or should he vote to build the new school immediately and delay the sewerage system?

# Study Guide for Case #16

To the Instructor and Student::

This guide is designed to assist the student in analyzing this case in the following ways. It suggests:

1. a major *Area of Educational Concern* that is central to the case and upon which the student should focus his/her research efforts.

2. *Concepts* that are related to key dimensions of the case and that the student should seek to understand. These *Concepts* have broad implications for educational theory and practice and are listed as *Pivotal Terms*.

3. *Questions* that are concerned with problems raised by the case and that the student should explore further for possible issues;

4. *Reference Material* that is related to the case and that the student should use as a resource in researching the case;

## Case #16

*"Abbeville's Dilemma"*

1. *Area of Educational Concern:* Should meeting the educational needs of our children take priority over meeting environmental, economic, or physical needs of our community?

2 *Concepts-Pivotal Terms:*

| | |
|---|---|
| "town and gown" activities | local control |
| GI Bill | extracurricular activities |
| property tax | double session |
| fixed-income retirees | accreditation |
| school plant maintenance | overcrowding |
| ground water | eutrophication |
| public health | phytoplankton |
| ecology | zooplankton |
| munincipal facilities | coliform |
| Environmental Protection Agency | runoff |
| land grant colleges | town meetings |

3. *Questions:*

What is the most equitable and effective way to raise money for the costs of public education?

Should there be local control over the operations and funding of schools?

Can double session provide an effective and meaningful educational experience?

Should there be local control over the construction and maintenance of sewerage systems?

What should be the relationship between a public college and the residents of the area where it is located?

How can school districts best prepare and provide for fluctuating demands for physical plant space created by the ever-changing size of a student population?

Should education and environmental issues be decided by popular referendum?

4. *Reference Material:*

Adams, E. Kathleen. (1982). The fiscal conditions of the states. *Phi Delta Kappan,* 63(9), 598–600.

Bakalis, Michael J. (1981). American education and the meaning of scarcity. *Phi Delta Kappan,* 63(2), 102–105.

Everett, David and Susan Kiernan. (1987). *Where the Land Meets the Water: A Citizen's Guide to Land Use.* Providence, RI: Save the Bay, Inc.

Garms, Walter I., Guthrie, James W., and Pierce, Lawrence C. (1978). *School Finance: The Economics and Politics of Public Education.* Englewood Cliffs, NJ: Prentice-Hall.

Papillon, Alfred L. and McGlinn, Patricia A. (1961). How well do pupils learn in double-shift classes? *Catholic School Journal,* 61(7), 66–67.

Pinkney, H. B. (1980). An American dilemma: Financing public education. *NASSP Bulletin,* 64(439), 68–73.

Reedy, Agnes Irene. (1959). Overcrowding and double session. *Grade Teacher,* 77(3), 150–151.